DORSET
FOLK
TALES

DORSET
FOLK TALES

TIM LAYCOCK

The History Press

First published 2012

The History Press
The Mill, Brimscombe Port
Stroud, Gloucestershire, GL5 2QG
www.thehistorypress.co.uk

Reprinted 2017

British Library Cataloguing in Publication Data.
A catalogue record for this book is available from the British Library.

ISBN 978 0 7524 6636 1

Typesetting and origination by The History Press
Printed in Great Britain by TJ Books Ltd, Padstow, Cornwall

CONTENTS

ACKNOWLEDGEMENTS

I have gathered these stories and songs during a lifetime of living, working and playing in Dorset, and very often when I retell the tales and sing the songs I can see and hear the person who gave the story to me. Several of these stories come from people who were recognised as storytellers and performers in their own communities, such at Netta Taylor at Uploders; but most are from people who would never regard themselves as storytellers, but who value the oral history, village memories and anecdotes of their family, village or area. Many of the stories were collected while working in day centres on projects for ArtCare and Artsreach – Dorset's Rural Touring Scheme; I would particularly like to thank Ian Scott and Angie Green of Artsreach, who supported two projects, one to collect stories in six Dorset villages, and the other, 'The Story Tree', to encourage and develop storytelling in the county. I have also spent a great deal of time performing stories in village halls, libraries and schools all over Dorset, and I would like to take this opportunity to thank the many teachers, librarians and village hall organisers who have helped to keep the oral history of Dorset alive; and to the audiences who have participated, often very actively, in these performances. The work that I have done in the county for Natural England, the Dorset Wildlife Trust, the National Trust and Dorset County Council has helped to contribute facts, stories and anecdotes to this collection – for this I thank you. I would also like to acknowledge the Sting in the Tale Festival of Storytelling, held in Dorset during August, which continues to do a great job in encouraging storytelling of all kinds in the county.

The staff at the Dorset County Museum and the Dorset History Centre have provided help and directed me to many interesting aspects of Dorset folk life, and I would like to thank them, especially Roger Peers, the former curator at the County Museum, and Jon Murden, the current director.

William Barnes and Thomas Hardy were both deeply interested in the folk life of Dorset, and several tales in this collection either influenced their writing or are derived from their poems and stories. I would like to thank all my friends in the William Barnes Society, the Thomas Hardy Society and the New Hardy Players for the support and inspiration that they have provided.

The songs in this book are mostly from the folk song collection of the Hammond Brothers – Robert and Henry – which is lodged with the English Folk Dance and Song Society. I would like to acknowledge the tremendous help and inspiration that I have always received from the staff at the Vaughan Williams Memorial Library at Cecil Sharp House: in particular the librarian, Malcolm Taylor. He is a real enthusiast for traditional music and has been instrumental in getting all the Hammond songs onto the Take 6 website, where they are available for anyone who is interested in the old songs of Dorset.

I would like to thank Michelle Tilly for the lovely illustrations she has provided for this book. Thanks also to Angela Laycock; Douglas Laycock; Dorothy Coombes;

Mr Chipp; Colin Thompson; John Hodgson; Pippa Brindley; Tracy Cooper; Lal Hitchcock; Christine Pfaff; Nancy Scott; Taffy Thomas; Sarah Harbige; Hannah Worthington; Sue Clifford and Angela King at Common Ground; and to all the people and places who have contributed tales and anecdotes to this collection. As William Barnes said:

> Why, tidden vields an' runnen brooks,
> Nor trees in Spring an' fall;
> An' tidden woody slopes an' nooks,
> Do touch us most of all;
> An' tidden ivy that do cling
> By housen big an' wold, O,
> But this is, after all, the thing,–
> The pleace a teale's a-twold o'

INTRODUCTION

Dorset is justly celebrated for its wonderfully varied landscapes, and the variety of stories, tales, legends and yarns to be found in the county is similarly diverse. I have been listening to legends, telling tales and making music in Dorset for many years now, and the stories here are a small selection of those told around the county. The oral tradition of stories, song, dance, customs and local lore still continues; after all, despite all the many and varied media attractions of the twenty-first century, there is nothing more compelling than a good tale well told. Many of the stories in this collection have been told to me at festivals, church events, village hall entertainments, even on street corners and of course, occasionally, in pubs. Particular mention should be made of the role of the Women's Institute in recording and keeping alive many fascinating stories, anecdotes and facts about village life in the area, that are very often stranger than fiction. In some cases the stories come originally from tellers of national repute such as Ruth Tongue; but mostly they are from Dorset folk who love their county and take a great interest in the past, present and future doings of their friends, acquaintances and former residents of their communities.

1

HORSE SENSE

There were these two old farmers; one was coming from Sturminster market in his trap, while the other was going in his cart, with two pigs under a net. They met on that narrow bridge in Hammoon (you know where I mean?) and they stopped. Whoooaa!

'Morning Benjamin,' said James.

'Mornin' James,' said old Ben.

'Tell me, Ben, when your horse had the staggers and the gaspings last November, what did 'ee give him?' asked the first farmer.

His neighbour replied, 'I give him an 'andful of ball bearings and a pint of axle oil.'

'Thank'ee Benjamin, much obliged,' said the first, as he whipped up his horse and went on his way.

Three weeks later they met on the same bridge. Whooaaa!

'Morning Benjamin,' said James.

'Mornin' James,' replied his neighbour.

'Now Ben, do 'ee remember last time we met, I asked you what you gave your horse when it had the staggers and the gaspings, and you said you give him a handful of ball bearings and a pint of axle oil?'

Ben replied that he did.

'Well,' says James indignantly, 'I done that, and my horse died!'

Ben looked at him in amazement, 'Well, blow me,' he exclaimed, 'that's queer! So did mine!'

Stories about horses are still commonplace in Dorset, even though the vast majority of farmwork nowadays is done by machinery. There are plenty of horses still to be seen in the county, although most of them are much lighter than the old workhorses used on the farms. There was always a certain mystique attached to the art of horsemanship, and the curing of equine ills. One very unusual tale about a horse with magical powers was told to Ruth Tongue by D. Barnett of Broadstone in 1928, when the majority of farmwork in Dorset was still horse- and steam-powered.

At one time there were orchards all over Dorset. Every village, every farm, had them. There was an old widow who lived down near Wareham, she had two orchards that produced wonderful apples every autumn; so many, that she had to get her friends and neighbours to come round to help pick them. They were the most delicious apples that anyone had ever tasted, and that's saying something. When she took them into Wareham market to sell them, she made enough money to keep her comfortable for the rest of the year.

This old widow was very old-fashioned, and kept up the old ways. Every night she would put out a bowl of cream and another of spring water, for she knew that there were those who guarded orchards, and she wanted to do right by them.

Some folk thought she put the cream out for the birds, or the hedgehogs, or the badgers that came snuffling through at night; but you and I know it was for Lazy Lawrence, a dainty little colt-pixie that lived in those parts. Strange name for such a lively creature really; he could run like the wind, and jump hedges as if they were only inches high. Very few people had ever seen him, but more than a few boys and girls had felt the nip of his teeth when they crope into orchards at night to scrump a few apples. You couldn't make the slightest sound if you wanted to scrump, because Lazy Lawrence would hear you and come at a gallop. Most importantly, whatever you did, you could never look into his eyes. Blazing green, they were, and if once he caught you in his gaze, you'd be transfixed to the spot until he pleased to let you go. That's why the older folk knew a rhyme that went:

Lazy Lawrence, let me go,
Don't make me wait an hour or so

Now it so happened there was an old conjuror lived on Purbeck, black-hearted old fella he was, and he'd heard about the old widow's apples. He decided to help himself, but being in the conjuring trade he knew all about Lazy Lawrence, and was wary of those green eyes and sharp teeth. So one night he climbed into a great apple hamper and conjured up a spell that sent the hamper tumbling into the middle of the orchard, and then another that sent all the widow's apples raining down onto the ground in a great circle, and some of 'em flying into the hamper itself. One particularly large one – a Warrior I believe – struck the old conjuror such a blow on his head that he yelled out, and that was his big mistake. Lazy Lawrence heard him, and was over the hedge and into the orchard in an instant, kicking the hamper all over the place, conjuror and all, and, when he tried to climb out, Lazy Lawrence caught him with those green eyes and made him stand still as a statue, surrounded by all the widow's apples.

Well, next morning – what a sight! There was the conjuror, unable to move, with all the apples in a great circle round him, and the hamper broken all to pieces. And round the apples they could clearly see a circle of hoofprints, so they knew 'twas Lazy Lawrence that had helped the widow. They could have called the conjuror all sorts of names, or slung mud at him, but they didn't, because they knew that would break the spell and the conjuror would have been free. Instead, they made him wait there until the dew was dried by the sun and the footprints disappeared; and then he was able to make his way, all kicked and bruised, off down the road towards Wareham. The folk all set to and brought baskets and pails for the widow's apples, took them into the market, and sold them for a very good price. Well, as they say:

An apple a day keeps the doctor away … and also the conjuror!

The Hobby Colt

I mind when I was a hobby colt, a hobby colt so gay,
And when my mother weaned me I thought that I should die,
Poor old horse, poor old horse.

I mind when I was a brewer's horse, a brewer's horse so gay,
I jumped right into the mashing tub and drank up all the beer

I mind when I was a gentleman's horse, a gentleman's horse
so gay,
I had the best of all the corn and the finest of the hay

This song was collected by Robert and Henry Hammond
from Beatrice Crawford, aged thirteen, at West Milton in
May 1906. The Hammonds collected hundreds of folk songs
in Dorset, and Beatrice seems to have been their youngest
informant – most of the singers were elderly people, including Beatrice's grandmother, who contributed eleven folk
songs, most of them old ballads.

2

MAURICE GREEN'S BLUE PIG

Every year at the Horticultural Show there was a competition for the finest pig in the village and every year since anyone could remember Maurice Green's pigs had won the prize, although Mrs Pike complained that her eldest daughter Susan should have won, because she was the greatest pig she'd ever known.

Anyway, Maurice had won so often, he came to regard the prize as his right and began to take it for granted, although this particular year he'd decided to improve his chances by getting some blue paint to smarten up the railings round the pigsty. Stratton's paint it was – best quality. Of course, he hadn't actually done it, but the paint was in the bucket, ready mixed.

Well, on the night before the revels Maurice went down to the Talbot to have his customary pint, and young Stacey was in there with some of his cronies, playing darts. Proper blabbermouth he was, so as soon as he sees Maurice he calls out, 'Hey Maurice, some of us got money on Tucker's pig for tomorrow!'

Well they tried to shut him up, but the cat was out of the bag. Oh yes, the damage was done.

'Tucker? Who's Tucker?'

'You know him, Maurice,' said the landlord, anxious not to aggravate one of his regulars; 'works for the parson; newish fella – only been in the village twelve years; lives in that cottage behind the recreation field.'

And then Maurice did something that the regulars in the Talbot had never seen before; he left his pint unfinished and walked out, saying ,'Right: I'm off to see Tucker's pig!'

Maurice went straight home. Mrs Green was surprised to see him back before closing time and said, 'Tucker's just been round here to see your pig; said it was a neighbourly call, as you was so famous for your pigs.'

'Tucker? What did he do? What did he say?'

'Not a lot: prodded her with a stick, sniffed and grunted, stirred his stick in your blue paint, and went on.'

'I'm off to see Tucker's pig,' says Maurice. Mrs Green was worried; she'd been married to Maurice for nigh on forty years, but they was a strange lot, the Greens, and she couldn't pretend to know exactly what he was thinking; but she could sense when there was trouble brewing.

Maurice went down the lane past the recreation field towards Tucker's house. Tucker saw him coming and snuck round the corner behind the shed. Mrs Tucker came out. 'Can I help you?' she said, nice as apple pie.

'I've come to see Tucker's pig,' says Maurice gruffly.

'Oh, she's in the sty, she's just been washed,' says Mrs Tucker.

Maurice went round, with Mrs Tucker following nervously. A huge porker lay resplendent on a bed of straw. Its skin shone, and a strange, sweet smell filled the air. Maurice sniffed suspiciously – he knew the smell, though he couldn't quite put his finger on it. 'What d'you wash him with?' he asked at last.

'Wright's Coal Tar Soap,' says Mrs T, 'and then finish off with baby powder!'

'Oh well, I suppose that's because you're incomers, and you don't know how we do things round here,' says Maurice. 'We always bed 'em down in lavender!' But his heart felt like a lump of lead; he knew he was in trouble. Without another word he turned and went straight home, and the first thing he said to his wife was 'Baby powder!'

'Don't be daft, Maurice,' says Mrs Green, 'you of all people should know we've had no call for that for twenty years!' But she could see he was upset, so she says, 'You go and wash the pig – here, use my Palmolive soap, and I'll get you some lavender.'

'We haven't got any!' says Maurice, nearly in tears.

'Don't you fret,' says his wife, 'Parson's got plenty; he won't miss a bunch or two.'

So Maurice went into the sty and looked at his pig, and somehow she seemed to have lost weight since that morning; and he washed her with missus' Palmolive soap, and dried her using missus' best tablecloth, but somehow his heart wasn't in it. Mrs Green came back with an armful of lavender and they bedded the pig down.

'Go to bed Maurice', she said, 'you'll feel better about it in the morning.' But she was worried; she never quite knew what he was thinking, and some of the Greens had curious ways. Some people even said they had the gift, and she was never quite sure they weren't right about that.

Well, later on that night, when his missus was sleeping sound, Maurice slipped quietly out of bed and tiptoed downstairs with boots in hand, so as not to make any noise. He let himself out, and walked quietly along the land past the recreation field to Tucker's. On the way he took his penknife and cut a hazel switch from the hedge. When he got there he took the switch and scratched a circle in the dust in front of the sty, and planted the stick in the middle. He meant to curse Tucker's pig, but in the end he couldn't quite do it; he couldn't bring himself to wish evil on another man's pig. Just then, St Mary's Church clock struck twelve midnight. All of a sudden the hazel switch came alive and started to tear around inside the circle like a wild thing. Maurice took to his heels and fled; he ran down the lane full pelt, up his steps and in through his own front door. He was in such a hurry that he kicked over the bucket of blue paint, but he didn't stop to clear it up, he just dived under the covers and there he stayed 'til morning.

Well, round about six in the morning there was the most tremendous knocking on the front door, and there was the milkman from Bartlett's farm: 'Maurice get up quick, get up, your pig's turned blue!'

Well it was true; the pig had rolled in the paint and was blue from head to foot. They did their best with the scrubbing brush and the carbolic, but 'twas all to no avail; Stratton's Best Paint did what it said on the tin – didn't come off in a hurry!

So Maurice Green's pig didn't win that year at the Horticultural Show; the judges didn't like the blue paint.

But neither did Tucker's pig, because the judges were very suspicious of the blue paint – the exact same colour as the pig – on his walking stick. In the end, they gave the prize to the parson's housekeeper. Her pig was only a little black runt, but they felt sorry for her because her lavender bushes were in such a poor state.

The belief that misfortune and sickness could be caused by the ill-wish of another person was widely held in Dorset until very recently. People who kept to old and reclusive ways were likely to be suspected of witchcraft, sympathetic magic or conjuring. William Barnes' poem 'A Witch' chronicles how the spell cast by an over-looker blights a farmer and his stock; and Thomas Hardy draws on local legends of conjurors and cunning men in *The Mayor of Casterbridge* and *The Withered Arm*. Many people who would not regard themselves as superstitious still take the sensible precaution of placing a horseshoe over the door, and avoid walking under ladders, or place a bowl of water or cream in the back garden or orchard for anyone that might need it. Plenty of people still believe that warts can be charmed away, either by the exchange of money or by rubbing the affected area with raw meat and then burying the meat, or by rubbing it with the inside of broad bean pods or banana skins. One old man in Stour Provost was known for charming warts. His method was to take a penny from the person afflicted, mutter some words, and bury the penny in the mortar of the church wall. Local children got to know of this and would dig out the pennies to spend on sweets!

3

THE THORNCOMBE THORN

Not many stories are completely new; most have their roots in other, earlier tales. But very few have such deep and vital roots as this one, reaching back to the Bible on the one hand and to the legends of King Arthur and the Knights of the Round Table on the other. If that isn't a sufficient pedigree, the story also gave a name to the village where it was recounted to me ten years ago by a retired gardener. We sat together in his small cottage on a dark October afternoon, and he showed me a photograph of himself as a fresh-faced apprentice gardener, sitting on a very ornate garden bench. This is Sonny's story of the history of that bench.

On the day after the crucifixion, the body of Christ was taken for burial in a tomb belonging to Joseph of Arimathea. Following the miracle of the Resurrection, Joseph was one of the first to see the empty tomb, and he subsequently travelled all over the world, telling the story of what he had seen with his own eyes. Some say he came to England, bringing with him the Holy Grail, the cup used by Christ and the disciples at the Last Supper. The Grail was lost or hidden somewhere in England, and was later to provide the ultimate quest for the Knights of King Arthur.

Joseph was an old man, and needed a staff to help him on his long journeys. His staff was made of rose thorn and when he came to the sacred site of Glastonbury in Somerset, he planted his staff in the ground and it immediately took root and blossomed, symbolising the new religion that had grown so successfully in the ancient sacred site. That thorn still flourishes in Glastonbury Abbey, thanks to generations of monks and gardeners who have maintained it; and it reputedly blossoms on Old Christmas Day, the day we now call 5 January.

As the fame of Glastonbury Abbey spread, pilgrims were attracted from all over the country, and many of the old green tracks became pilgrimage routes. To help show the way, the monks planted cuttings from the Glastonbury rose, and one such marker was planted in Thorncombe by the monks from Forde Abbey. It became such a recognised site that a settlement grew up around the rose, and has been known ever since as Thorncombe.

Many hundreds of years later the thorn was still growing, although now enclosed in the garden of a wealthy local landowner who lived in what is now Sedbergh Hall. Sedbergh was owned by the Wragge family, and was at the time a beautiful and ancient old home, full of character and cobwebs. The eldest son of the family fell in love with Lucie, the daughter of the portrait painter Thomas Gainsborough. The Gainsborough connection with the area can still be seen in the name and sign of the inn at Clacton, the Blue Boy, named after Gainsborough's famous portrait. Miss Gainsborough informed her hopeful lover that on no account would she marry him unless he demolished the old manor house and built a new one in the then current style.

John Wragge worked as a vintner in London, and one day he was leaning over London Bridge, contemplating the river below and wondering how he might ever make enough money to rebuild his family home and win the woman he loved, when he overheard a curious conversation. Two men were talking, and what made John listen was that they mentioned the name of Thorncombe – his home village. He listened more closely, and heard one tell the other that beneath the roots of the old rose thorn in Thorncombe there was gold and silver buried, a treasure trove there for the taking.

Well, John Wragge wasted no time. He set off straight away on horseback and galloped all the way to Thorncombe, where he ordered the roots of the thorn to be carefully exposed; and sure enough, there was the treasure, enough to rebuild the house and keep his bride in the manner to which she was accustomed.

Such is the romantic story about the building of Sedbergh Hall; although some have unkindly suggested that it is all a fabrication designed to divert attention from rather more dubious commercial dealings in the past.

The rose was cherished in the garden for many generations, right into the twentieth century, when a young local chap was taken on as under-gardener at Sedbergh Hall. At last the venerable rose died, and the branches were fashioned into a rustic seat and placed in the garden. That young man was photographed on the seat and he passed on the history of the Thorncombe thorn to me, and now I have told it to you.

4

THE BEGGARS' WEDDING

No one knew how old Doll was. It seemed as if she'd always been there; sometimes sitting, sometimes with a basket of lucky heather, occasionally picking out a tune on a whistle or a broken fiddle, always with a song of some sort to offer. And because people knew her, they would sometimes give a few pence, or buy her a sandwich or a drink, though it could never have been enough to keep her going. Quite how she survived no one really knew.

But Doll had a big secret, and illustrious ancestors. She was the last in a long line of Dolls, stretching right back to the time of the first Queen Bess, when the foreign wars made lots of soldiers lame or blind, and their grateful country, glad enough to see them in front of the enemy cannons and pikes, was not caring enough to provide any means of sustenance for them on their return. Instead they took to the roads in packs and tribes, marching from town to town, displaying their lameness, blindness and wounds and begging for alms. As time passed, some of these beggars became so used to their roving, precarious existence that they had no desire to settle down, and became so adept at the 'mumping' trade that they grew quite wealthy on it. This naturally attracted the envy of others, who debased the trade by faking wounds and injuries so that after a time a Good Samaritan could not be sure whether he or she was helping a real beggar or a counterfeit one.

Doll had no affliction of her own; her beggary was hereditary; she regarded it as the family business as much as a baker or a cobbler. A long line of Dolls had worked as she worked, and one of the tools of her trade was an old ballad. Composed by one of the tribe, she would sing it everywhere she went – as much for her own entertainment as to raise money, for certainly the tune was doleful enough, and the song so long, that very few bothered to pause and listen, even if they could have interpreted the woman's thick accent. But the story she told was remarkable and spoke of a happier time for the beggars, when they were briefly the toast of the county and their sense of morality was deemed to be higher than that of the local gentry.

The substance of the ballad was this:

All you that delight in a jest that is true
Give ear to these lines I unfold to you …

Years ago there was a well-respected knight in Dorsetshire. He and his wife were blessed with a beautiful baby daughter, and she was their pride and joy. The knight's neighbour and closest friend was a rich merchant, and he and his wife were the proud parents of a tiny son, exactly the same age as the knight's daughter. The knight and his wife enjoyed good health, but the merchant and his wife were both stricken with a sickness, and when the two children were only three years old, the merchant and his wife were near to death. The merchant called in his friend, and spoke earnestly to him.

'I know that I am dying,' he said. 'I beg you, my dearest friend, to look after my young son when we are gone, and raise him as one of your family.'

The knight promised faithfully that he would fulfil his friend's wish.

'Furthermore,' said the dying man, 'my dearest wish would be that my son might marry your daughter, and I will leave all my lands and riches to them both to ensure their health and happiness in time to come.'

The knight happily agreed to this generous offer, but made the practical point that the merchant's son might die before reaching manhood; and what should happen then?

'In that case,' said the merchant, 'all my wealth shall come to you, old friend, for the kindness that you have shown to my family and me.'

The knight sorrowfully agreed to these conditions and a few days later the merchant and his wife died at exactly the same time on the same day, and were buried in one grave together; true lovers to the end. The knight took the young boy Jemmy into his own household, and for a few years he honoured his dead friend's memory and looked after the boy as his own son.

So Jemmy and the knight's daughter Susannah grew up together and were inseparable. Their delight in each other's company was plain for all to see, and the beauty of both children impressed all who saw them. But gradually the knight began to think that perhaps his daughter was too beautiful and too high-born to marry a merchant's son; and in time he convinced himself that not only would it be a misfortune for his daughter, but that it was his duty as a responsible parent to make a better match for Susannah. The knight became completely obsessed with this idea until, at last, he resolved to have Jemmy killed, so that he could claim the merchant's money and allow his daughter to marry a more suitable husband.

It happened that the tribe of beggars came into Dorsetshire shortly afterwards, which gave the knight his opportunity.

He sent his manservant to seek out a beggar who might be prepared to assist a gentleman to remove an impediment, no questions asked; for which service a large amount of money would be paid. A beggar was duly found and instructed in his duties. The following day the knight walked out into the garden, where Jemmy and Susannah were happily playing together, and invited the boy to come for a walk and take the air. The little girl wanted to come too, but her father forbade her and sent her indoors. Then the knight called in the beggar, dressed in fine clothes so as not to arouse the boy's suspicions, saying, 'This is my manservant John; he will take you for a walk and show you many fine things, and later on you can play with Susannah again.'

The young boy dutifully went off with the disguised beggar and they walked for many miles, the child innocently chattering away to the beggar. After a while, however, Jemmy began to miss his playmate, and asked the beggar where they were going. The beggar relented from his cruel mission and decided instead to let Jemmy live; he took the child back to his wife Doll to raise as their own.

When Doll saw the boy and heard the tale she was delighted. 'He's a well-favoured boy,' she said, 'I like him; he can go a-begging with us!'

At first the boy was happy in his strange new home; but soon he began to pine for his playmate, and the beggar decided that it would be natural justice if he was to steal the knight's daughter and bring her to live with the beggars too. Accordingly, he walked back into Dorset one dark night, stole up to the knight's hall, and carried off the sleeping girl in a blanket. Along the road Doll was waiting, and they stripped off her fine clothes, flung them over a hedge, and dressed her as a beggar. By daybreak they were miles away, hidden amongst the community of beggars, and Jemmy was reunited with Susannah.

When the knight found his daughter was gone, he was distraught. He raised a hue and cry in every town in the county and offered a reward of £5,000 to the man or woman who might find the girl; but all that could be found were her clothes, discarded in a field, which convinced the knight that his daughter was dead.

Then the greedy knight had cause to repent, and he bitterly mourned the loss of his child. 'This is all my own fault,' he said to himself, 'I have brought the wrath of Heaven on my own head for daring to take a life for my own purposes; and now I have lost the thing I held most precious, the joy of my heart.'

Meanwhile, far away, Jemmy and Susannah were happy together with their new parents, and very readily took to the mumping trade. With their beautiful looks and pleasant ways they were very successful as beggars, and the beggar and his wife were delighted. One day he said to his wife, 'Wife, I have an idea, which I hope you will indulge for me, and it is this: that the money I was paid to kill Jemmy shall become a wedding portion for him, and I will give twice as much more, and when the two of them are eighteen they shall be married in the finest beggars' wedding that ever was known!'

Well, Doll was so delighted with this plan that she clapped her hands and kissed her husband, and declared it was the best idea he'd ever had, and he'd had quite a few. 'Yes,' said the beggar, 'and we'll have a score of handsome beggars to accompany Jemmy as suitors, and we'll give out the news that there's to be a real beggars' wedding, and we'll do it in Dorchester.'

'Perfect,' says Doll, 'we'll have the best of food and drink!'

'Yes,' says the beggar, 'and if the knight is still living, he shall come along, and I'll make him a present of his daughter once she's lawfully wed to Jemmy, which no man can put asunder!'

Well, Doll was so excited she declared she could hardly wait, but as the children were not yet ten, she had no choice.

So, for eight years they rambled all over the West Country, mumping as they went.

At last, the day of the wedding arrived. The whole tribe of beggars were determined to make it the best wedding ever seen. Money was found in pots and buried boxes and bags, and fine clothes were bought for bride and groom. The clothes were made even finer by sewing on gold and silver coins all over, until they shone like the stars. A great procession was formed, bride and groom in front, twenty suitors next, and all the rest of the begging tribe behind. In this way they sang and danced their way into Dorset, and all the time news of the beggars' wedding spread far and wide.

As the party came into Dorchester great crowds assembled, amazed at the beauty and splendour of the bride and groom and their outlandish attendants and guests. The beggars requested food and drink for the wedding feast, and great quantities of mouldy cheese, rusty bacon and noggins of ale were freely donated. The finest and largest room in the town was hired so that as many as possible could see the wedding, and the clamour for seats amongst high and low was insatiable; everyone wanted to see the beggars' wedding.

The knight was now an old man, gloomy and sad. His wife had died some years before, and his life was cold and empty. But he heard his servants talking about the beggars' wedding, so he called his man to saddle his horse, and set off for Dorchester to see the spectacle.

When the knight came into the hall, the wedding ceremony and feast were already over. Jemmy and Susannah were man and wife, the food was all eaten and the drink was nearly gone. The piper was playing his pipes, and the bride and her friends were dancing a hey. The hall shook with joy and laughter, and even the morose old knight felt his

spirits lift. He looked idly at the laughing bride, and something about her sent a shiver through him – he thought he
recognised her, but he couldn't be sure. Then the bride got
up to dance, and Doll called on the piper for a jig, which
she danced with such grace that the entire company was
transfixed. Then the beggar, bursting with pride and not to
be outdone, called on the piper for a hornpipe for his son.
'My friends,' he cried, 'a health to the bridegroom! Though
he's a beggar's son brought up, he's a merchant's son by
birth!'

Then the knight, his heart pounding, stepped up to the
bride, bowed low, and begged her to listen to him. 'If you
have the mark of a rose on your breast, I vow and declare
that you are my only daughter, who for thirteen years I have
thought dead.'

> She showed him the mark, he immediately cried
> Take home the bridegroom and the sweet bride!
> For this is my joy that's been missing so long,
> And her dear joy, the merchant's young son.

He promised that he would receive them kindly if they
would come to his hall, and invited the whole company to
come, to see that he kept his word and confessed his guilt.
The beggars' ran through the town, shouting the joyful
news that true love and virtue had triumphed, and everyone
praised the beggar who had saved the boy's life.

But, although the knight was reunited with his daughter, he could never remove the stain of the deed that he had
intended to be done. Not long afterwards he died, leaving
the young couple £6,000 a year for life. Old Doll and her
husband went to live with Jemmy and Susannah, and as far
as we know they all lived happily ever after.

Leaving old Doll with the last words, which have been repeated by other Dolls right down to the present day:

> You misers that are of a covetous mind
> Strive not to prevent what the powers designed

The Beggars' Wedding can be found in verse form in J.S. Udal's *Dorsetshire Folk-Lore*.

Poor Jolly Sailor Lads

> Come all you jolly sailors a line to you I'll write,
> In ploughing of the ocean I take a great delight:
> The landsmen fear no danger, no danger do they know,
> While we poor jolly sailor lads plough the wide ocean through.
>
> When labouring men come home at night they tell the girls fine tales
> What they have been a-doing all in the new corn fields
> 'Tis a-cutting of the grass so high is all that they can do
> While we poor jolly sailor lads plough the wide ocean through
>
> He's the night as black as any pitch, and the wind begins to blow
> Our captain he commands us – All hands turn out below
> Our Captain he commands us our goodly ship to guard
> Jump up aloft my lively lads and strike top-gallant yards
>
> You see a storm a-rising, and we are all confound
> Expecting every moment that we shall all be drowned
> Cheer up Cheer up my lively lads we shall see out homes again
> In Spite of all our dangers, we'll plough the raging main

And when the wars are over, and we are safe on shore

We'll drink and we will sing my boys as we have done before

We'll drink and we will sing my boys and spend our money free

And when our money is all gone, we'll boldly go to sea.

This song was sung to the Hammond brothers by Joseph Elliott in Todber. As a young man he had journeyed with fifty other Dorset men down to Dartmouth in Devon, to sail to Newfoundland to work on the cod fishery. Many of the songs and ballads that he sang must have been learnt during his years at sea.

5

JACK AND THE BOAT

You know Jack don't you? He was the one who climbed up the beanstalk and stole the golden goose from the giant. But what you might not know was that Jack had two brothers, Bill and Tom, and the three of them were always trying to outdo each other; and because Jack was the youngest, he had to be clever to outdo the strength of his older brothers.

However, some days they did agree, and one thing that all agreed was that they wanted to be fishermen, so one day they went to their mother and asked her to buy them a boat.

'A boat?' she said, 'D'you think I'm made of money? I can't afford to buy a boat for you boys! If you want a boat, you'll have to make it yourselves; go up to the woods and cut down trees. But I will help you; I'm going to bake three special buns each for you boys, and those buns will be full of energy, so you can work all day in the woods chopping down trees for your boat. You must promise me you'll eat those buns.'

Well, the three of them did promise, and the following morning up goes Tom to the woods with an axe and a saw. Now Tom was the eldest and the strongest, and by lunchtime he had five great trees laid out on the ground. Tom sat on one, had a cup of tea, and began to eat one of the special buns his mother had made for him. He was just about to sink his teeth into the second bun when he noticed a very old lady sitting on the end of the tree trunk. The old lady looked at Tom and said, 'Well done Tom, that's good work; you must be very strong to cut down so many trees. Can you spare me one of those buns you're eating?'

Well, Tom remembered what his mother had said, so he replied, 'I'm really sorry I can't. I promised my mother I would eat them, for energy; I've got a lot of work to do here.'

'That doesn't matter Tom, that's fine, but you will get your reward,' said the old lady and then she just disappeared, which was strange. But Tom finished off the buns, sharpened up his axe and went back into the woods. He chose a great tall tree and swung his axe at it, but the tree shattered just as if it was made of glass; and so did the next one, and the next. In the end he gave up and went home, and told his mother what had happened.

'Well, never mind, let's see how Bill gets on tomorrow,' said their mother, and Bill gave a lopsided grin and reckoned it wouldn't be hard to do better than Tom. His older brother just glared at him.

Early next morning up goes Bill to the woods, and at first he was cautious, because he didn't want to get cut by any glass trees. But it was fine; the trees had all gone back to wood, and so Bill worked away all morning. By lunchtime there were four more great trees laid on the ground alongside the five that Tom had felled the previous day. Bill sat on one, had a cup of tea, and began to eat one of the special buns his mother had made for him. He was just about to sink his teeth into the second bun when he noticed a very old lady sitting on the end of the tree trunk. The old lady looked at Bill and said, 'Well Bill, that's pretty good work; you must be very strong to cut down so many trees. Can you spare me one of those buns you're eating?'

Well, Bill remembered what his mother had said so he replied, 'I'm really sorry I can't. I promised my mother I would eat them, for energy. There's a boat to be built, I've got a lot of work to do here.'

'Don't worry, that doesn't matter at all Bill, that's fine; but you will get your reward,' said the old lady and then she just disappeared, which was curious. But Bill finished off the buns, sharpened up his axe and went back into the woods.

He chose a great tall tree and swung his axe at it; but this time it didn't shatter like glass; this time his axe jumped back at him, and the whole tree rang like a bell. He tried another, and another, but it was no good; every tree in the wood had turned into hard iron, and all Bill did was blunt his axe. In the end there was nothing to do but go home and tell his mother what had happened.

'Well then, it's all down to Jack,' she said. Tom and Bill just laughed because, to tell you the truth, Jack was the smallest and the weakest of the three brothers, and it was all he could do to drag the axe up to the woods. When he finally got there he was very careful, because he didn't want to blunt the axe on an iron tree or get cut by a glass tree. But it was fine; the trees had all turned to wood again, and all morning Jack hacked away at a slender little tree until just before lunch, when he managed to bring it down. And he sat on that tree, had a cup of tea, and began to eat one of his mother's buns. He was just about to sink his teeth into the second bun when he noticed the same old lady sitting on the end of the tree trunk. The old lady looked at Jack and said, 'Well Jack, that's quite a good tree; can you spare me one of those buns you're eating?'

Well, Jack remembered what his mother had said, but he looked at the old lady and he felt sorry for her. He felt pretty full himself already, so he thought that really, it wouldn't hurt to give one of the buns to the old lady, so he did. And the two of them sat there, munching away on the buns in the middle of the wood. When the buns were finished, the old lady said to Jack, 'Now Jack, you helped me and I'll help you. What are you doing? Why have you cut down all these trees?'

So, Jack told the old lady all about the boat, and how he and his bothers wanted to be fishermen, and then she said, 'Well, how will you turn these trees into a boat? What do you do?'

And Jack explained about splitting the trees and planking them, and laying the keel and the ribs, and shaping the sides of the boat. And the old lady said, 'Right, Jack, you go into the woods and cut down one more tree for the mast, and I'll see what I can do.' And Jack thought to himself that it was not very likely that an old lady would be much help at boatbuilding, but he kept that thought to himself, and went off to cut down another tree.

When he came back a couple of hours later he was amazed – there, in the middle of the wood, was the complete framework of a wooden boat: keel, ribs and all. 'What's next?' asked the old lady.

'Well, you have to nail the planks on the ribs, put on the deck, step the mast, raise the spars, rig the ropes, tie up the sails, put the anchor on the bow and the wheel astern.'

'Well, you just cut down one smallish tree for a flagpole, and I'll see what I can do,' said the old lady; and off went Jack into the woods.

When he came back, he was astonished to see that the boat was finished – planks, decks, mast rigging and sails all in place and shipshape. 'It's fabulous, thank you so much!'

'What's next?' said the old lady. And Jack told her that the only thing left to do was to paint the boat, and the old lady gave Jack a paintbrush.

'Thank you, but I shall need paint,' he said, but the old lady told him just to try the brush. When he set it to the side of the boat a red stripe came out, and as he walked round the ship, the colour changed to yellow, then blue, then gold, until that boat looked like a rainbow. And Jack thanked the old lady very much, but said there's just one problem; and when the old lady asked what the problem was, he said, 'It's this; this boat is in the middle of a wood, fifteen miles from the sea – how are we going to get her into the water?'

Then the old lady told Jack that it was a magic boat. If he got in and sang that old sailor song 'Hooray and Up She Rises', the boat would rise up and fly north, east, west or south. It could go under the sea like a submarine or up into the sky like a spaceship. It would even go back into the past or forwards into the future – wherever he told it to go.

'But if ever you want to land, Jack, you must remember this special word – Pitch! – and the boat will settle down and let you go off for an adventure.'

Then Jack thanked the old lady, got into the boat and set off on his travels – and if we had a month, I could tell you just a few of the places that Jack sailed to in the magic boat. But just for now I'll tell you how the tale ended. Jack looked down and there below him was a castle, so he said 'Pitch!' and down went the magic boat, and landed in the castle moat.

The king rushed out and shook Jack by the hand and he said, 'Jack, that's the best boat I've ever seen; you're such a fine fellow, I'd like you to marry my beautiful daughter!'

Just then out came the beautiful daughter, but she said she would not marry Jack just because he had a painted boat;

she would only marry him if he could play a decent hornpipe on a melodeon. Poor Jack was in despair, because he didn't even have a melodeon, let alone the ability to play one. But then he remembered he was in a magic boat, and he looked under the seat, and, sure enough, there was a melodeon. He took out the instrument and found he could play it straight away! And the princess began to dance. She danced down the steps of the castle, across the drawbridge and into the boat, and together they flew off and had many more extraordinary adventures.

But even that wasn't quite the end of the story. Jack began to get homesick, and he thought how much he would like to see his mother again; and when he looked down, there was his mother's house, and there were Bill and Tom and his mother standing by the stream waving. So he said 'Pitch!' and down went the boat and landed in the stream. Bill and Tom came up and hauled Jack out of the boat (the princess got out too) and they climbed in and demanded to know how to make the boat fly.

'It's easy,' said Jack, 'you just sing that old song that all sailors know, "Hooray and Up She Rises", and off you go!' So they began to sing, and off they went, but they'd been too hasty and forgotten to ask how to make the boat come down. So, as far as I know, they are still flying around in the boat to this very day!

Well, Jack's mother invited her prodigal son and the princess in for some food. She got out a tin table and piled it high with food and drink; but she put so much on that the tin table bended, so this story's ended.

I first heard a version of this story in Newfoundland. It was collected from a storyteller called William Pitman, who called it 'Jack and the Beautiful Punt'. There are very strong links between Dorset and Newfoundland, based on the cod fishing that formerly took place on the Grand Banks and other fishing grounds in the area. Poole was the centre for the trade in Dorset. Several merchant families in the town ran big enterprises that involved fleets of ships, large warehouses and a triangular trade that sent vessels, men and stores to Newfoundland. The cod was dried and salted, packed into barrels, and taken south to European countries, particularly Italy and Spain. The final leg of the journey was to bring back olive oil, wine and salt from the Mediterranean countries. Many of the largest houses in Poole were built on the profits of this trade, and a lot of Dorset men went to Newfoundland to work on the cod fishery. Quite a number settled on the island, and today Newfoundlanders trace their ancestry to three main sources: Dorset, Devon and Ireland. There are communities in Newfoundland where Dorset surnames such as Pitman are common, and you can still hear recognisably West Country accents. It was, of course, a two-way process, and many of the Dorset fishermen got married in Newfoundland and brought their brides back to live in England. One of the most significant Dorset folk singers, Joseph Elliott from Todber, worked in the cod fishery as a young man, and his lively repertoire of fishing and sea songs reflects this adventurous stage of his life. The men and women who settled in Newfoundland took their songs, stories and dance tunes with them, and today the traditional music and culture of the island is a heady mix of Devon, Dorset and Irish, with a strong dash of transatlantic flair!

The early years of the nineteenth century were the heyday for Newfoundland trade. At that time, the main Poole companies had agents in towns such as Blandford and Sturminster, who would recruit men and boys to go to sea. At a time when work on the land was poorly paid, it was an attractive alternative, and also a way of finding employment for workhouse boys. That's how this next story starts …

6

JACK AND THE
COFFEE MILL

This is the story of young Jack Fudge, who lived in Bagber, near Sturminster Newton. His father was a farmworker and died in an accident when the boy was only three, and his mother died of fever shortly afterwards, so the boy was brought up by his grandmother in Stur. The old lady had a bit put by, and a little cottage of her own, so she was able to send the boy to the school down by St Mary's Church, and look after him pretty well. Jack lived with his grandmother quite happily until he was ten years old. But eventually the old lady's health began to fail, and she knew in her heart that it wouldn't be long before she died, so one day she called Jack in to speak to him.

'Now then Jack, one day quite soon I will die, and you will have to make your own way in the world. I've raised you as best I can since your poor mother and father died, and I'm going to give you something to make sure you make a good start in life.'

Well, Jack was imagining gold or silver, but it wasn't any of those things. The old lady pointed to a battered old chest in the corner of the room.

'I've told you before, Jack, that my dear departed husband was a sailor; he was captain of a sailing ship, and sailed all round the world many times. That was his sea chest, and in his time he brought me home some strange and curious things. Open the chest, boy.'

Jack did as he was told and looked in. There was a telescope, a brightly coloured shawl, several old books, and a small package.

'Take out the package,' commanded the old lady. Jack picked it up. It fitted snugly in his two hands, and felt solid and heavy. 'Unwrap it,' she said. He untied the string and removed the oilcloth. Inside was a small, circular object with a handle on top.

'What is it?' he asked.

'It's a coffee mill,' she said.

Jack was disappointed. He didn't see at all how a small coffee mill could give him a good start in life. His grandmother smiled; she could tell what he was thinking. 'This is a special coffee mill Jack,' she said. 'Whatever you ask for, it will make it for you. If you want bread, all you have to do is say "Coffee mill, coffee mill, grind me bread", and it will do so. But it will keep on grinding until you say "Coffee mill, coffee mill, I thank you; no more bread". And you must always use that exact form of words – anything else, and the mill will not work, or it will continue to grind, and you won't be able to stop it.'

Jack looked at the mill with new respect, and thanked his grandmother. 'Can I try it?'

'Not now. You should only use it when you really need it. And don't tell anyone else that you have it, for someone will surely try to steal it from you. It's yours Jack; keep it a secret, and never let anyone else know about it.'

So Jack put the coffee mill away in the chest, and almost forgot about it. Then a few months later his grandmother died, and Jack had nowhere to go. He was too young to live on his own, so he was taken in by the parish and put in the workhouse.

The master looked at Jack and he said, 'Now look here, young Fudge, this is no place for you – a healthy, strapping lad like you. I've a mind to find you a place at sea, like your grandfather; would you like that?'

Well, Jack didn't want the workhouse any more than the workhouse wanted him, so he agreed to the master's suggestion. At that time there was an office in Stur for the Poole shipping, and the master took Jack down there. By the end of the day, he had signed on to sail for two winters and three summers to Newfoundland, and to fish on the Grand Banks as boy for Lesters, one of the biggest companies involved in the trade. There was a wagon going down to the coast with bales of swanskin later that week, and it was arranged that the boy would go too.

So it was that the following week Jack was on Poole Quay, waiting to be taken on-board a Newfoundland-bound sailing ship by the name of *The Elisabeth Jane*. He had his grandfather's sea chest to sit on; it already bore the name Fudge in tiny nailed letters, and Jack had taken out the nails that read James and replaced them to read Jack.

'Hey boy, looking for a ship?' A tall, bearded man, looking every inch a sailor, was standing over him, grinning.

'Oh, yes sir, I'm expected. Jack Fudge, sir: I've got my papers here …'

'Never mind about papers, lad, this is yer ship. On-board with ye!' And with that, he was bundled on-board a battered-looking vessel, just as the ropes were being cast off and the sails shaken out. 'Come on,' said the sailor, 'down below; I'll show you yer cabin!' and he pushed him down a ladder into a cabin, banged the door shut and bolted it from outside. The ship set sail, and that was the last that Jack ever saw of the port of Poole.

So that was how Jack came to be shanghaied and taken off to sea not with Lesters, but with a crew of the biggest rogues that ever sailed. There wasn't a man among them who wasn't on the run from something or other, or who hadn't committed some unspeakable crime. Cruel hard men they were, disappointed in life and determined to get what they wanted by any means. Worst of all was the captain, who ruled over them all by terror and fear, and kept discipline amongst his crew of jailbirds by killing any man that opposed him. Jack was the only boy on-board, and they all treated him abominably. He was made to do all the dirtiest, most menial tasks; he was abused and beaten on a daily basis, and he was fed only the few scraps that the sailors would not even deem suitable for the rats that swarmed everywhere below deck.

Yet despite this appalling treatment, Jack didn't appear to mind. He always had a smile on his face, he never complained, and he even appeared to like the life. The sailors were amazed, and rather puzzled. One night, when Jack was fast asleep in the tiny cubbyhole in the bows of the ship, the men sat around their mess table drinking grog, and yarning, and they began to discuss the strange young lad that they had on-board.

'He don't complain,' said one. 'You've got to grant him that; he don't say a word.'

'True,' said another. 'And I believe I even heard him singing a song the other day!'

'I give him a good larruping yesterday for not lashing up a reef properly, and he never flinched,' said the mate. 'Aye, he's a strange one, all right.'

'The strangest thing of all about him to my mind is his vittles,' said the cook. 'We never give him anything; yet look at him – rosy red cheeks, and fat as a pig!'

'What say we find out how he does it?' said the mate. 'I've a mind to squint in through that doorway yonder and see what I can spy.'

The rest of the crew kept up their carousing while the mate stole over to the cubby door. Peeping in, he saw the boy on his knees at the sea chest. He saw him take out the coffee mill and speak to it, and the mill began to grind. Before the mate's astonished gaze, a loaf of bread, a fine cheese and a can of grog appeared. Then the mill stopped grinding. The boy ate the food and drank the drink, blew out the stub of candle in his lantern, climbed into his hammock and went to sleep.

The mate could not decide what to do at first. He merely said that there was nothing to be seen when his shipmates questioned him; but when they had all retired, he called the cook back and told him what he'd seen. Together, they decided to offer the boy money for the coffee mill, because they could both see how it might make their fortunes.

Accordingly, the next night, when the crew were up on deck shortening sail in the teeth of a gale, the mate and the cook entered Jack's cabin, and offered him ten guineas for his coffee mill. The boy was frightened but obstinate; he refused to sell, even when the sailors increased their offer to twenty guineas.

'Well never mind, lad; you think about it,' said the mate, as pleasantly as he could. 'If you change yer mind, Jack, ye can let us know, eh Cookie?'

Later that night, when Jack was fast asleep, the mate and the cook silently entered the cubbyhole, knocked him unconscious with a single blow from a belaying pin, opened the port and threw him into the sea. They took the coffee mill and returned in triumph to the mess room.

The cook went off to serve up the soup. As usual, it was tasteless and thin.

'This is terrible,' said the mate. 'What we need is – salt!' and he looked around, grinned at his messmates, picked up the coffee mill and set it on the table, saying, 'Coffee mill, coffee mill, grind me salt!'

As the sailors watched the handle began to turn, and out came salt. They all crowed and cheered, sprinkling the salt into their soup and drinking their grog. The mate told them they were all rich – the mill would grind whatever they desired. The celebration became wilder and wilder; one of the sailors sprang onto the table and danced a hornpipe, and the rest beat time with their bowls and spoons. But in the melee the coffee mill was knocked under the table, still grinding out salt.

It was only an hour later, when the sailors were completely drunk and the cabin was knee-deep in salt, that they realised what was happening. They scrabbled around on the ground but couldn't find the mill, and at last they were forced out of the cabin and up on to deck by the salt, and still the mill kept turning. Before long the ship began to heel on one side and, as day broke, it turned over and slipped beneath the waves, with the loss of all hands. Still the coffee mill kept turning, eighty fathoms down on the ocean bed in the barnacle-encrusted ribs of that battered schooner; and it's still turning to this very day – and that's why the sea is salty. And if you taste it, you'll see what I mean!

Sometimes truth can be stranger than fiction. The *Mountaineer* was an 87-ton sloop built in Hamworthy in 1836. In 1850 she was found adrift 150 miles off Labrador with a cargo of salt, but no crew. The only possessions left on-board were three miniature portraits of Princess Alice, found in the captain's locker. The disappearance of the entire crew was never adequately explained, and no one ever came forward to say why the ship had come to be abandoned in such a way.

7

THE PORTLAND QUARRYMAN

Walter White was a quarryman, working away in a stone quarry high up on Portland, chipping away at the rock, doing the same work that he'd done year in, year out since he was a lad. He worked steadily and methodically, but his heart wasn't in it. He felt stuck – stuck on the island, and stuck in the same trade that his father and his father before him had followed. He wanted to be something different, someone more important.

Then he heard the sound of music floating across Weymouth Bay beneath him, and he looked up and towards the beach, where he could just make out a crowd of people, down at the water's edge. When he looked more closely he could see that it was King George, about to take his morning dip in the sea. There was the sun glinting on the king's crown; there was the bright white bathing machine, and all the flunkeys in their red and gold livery fussing around, and the king's German guards keeping back the admiring crowds. Then the band struck up 'God Save the King', and everyone cheered as the royal personage emerged from the bathing machine on the seaward side, took off his purple bathing robe and majestically entered the briny. The quarryman saw all this, and he thought to himself, 'He's important, he's powerful. I wish I could be like that – I wish I was the king.'

And suddenly there was a clap of thunder, and a sound just like a mighty fanfare on the biggest organ in the world, and the quarryman felt something heavy on his head. He reached up slowly, and realised to his amazement that it was a solid gold crown. Over his shoulders, in place of his moleskin jacket, was a rich red cloak with a great fur collar; and in his hand, in place of his hammer and chisel, an orb and sceptre. All the other quarrymen went down on their knees, crying, 'God save King Walter!', and even his boss, who had never been known to say a civil word to anyone on the island, bowed low and welcomed him humbly to the quarry. And the quarryman thought to himself, 'This is wonderful! Now I'm important, now I'm powerful; I am the KING!'

Well, for several years he had the time of his life. But one day, as he rode in his carriage through the streets of Wyke, the sun came out and shone down on the country below. All the crowds that had been cheering King Walter turned away and began to sunbathe and swim in the sea. Well, Walter thought to himself, 'Now wait a minute; the sun up in the sky is more powerful and important even than the king. See how everyone worships the sun. The centre of the universe; nothing is more important than the sun – I wish I was the sun!'

And suddenly there was a clap of thunder, and a sound just like a mighty fanfare on the biggest organ in the world, and the quarryman felt his robes disappear, and he was shooting up into the sky, growing hot and fiery and bright, until he took his rightful position up amongst the moons and stars and planets. He was the sun, beaming down light and heat and warmth onto the earth below, and he thought, 'This is it!

Now I'm powerful, now I'm important! Nothing can live without me! I'm the SUN!'

For years he was content, bringing life and light to the world below, revolving in space in stellar company. But then one day a cloud floated between him and the earth below, and the people began to get up, put on their clothes, put up their umbrellas and run indoors, and he thought to himself, 'Wait a minute; this cloud can block out my light and heat, so it must be more powerful and more important than myself – I wish I was a cloud!'

And suddenly there was a clap of thunder, and a sound just like a mighty fanfare on the biggest organ in the world, and the quarryman felt something clammy and cold around him. Swirling mist, great heavy drops of moisture, and electrical charges fizzing through his body, and he thought, 'This is fine! Now I'm powerful, now I'm important; I'm a THUNDERCLOUD!' And as he spoke the words, he flashed lightning down onto the world below, and rolled out great peals of thunder, and cascaded great storms of rain onto the earth.

But as he revelled in the power of the deluge he had created, he looked down and saw a stream, that quickly became a river, and then grew to a torrent and rampaged through the land, sweeping aside buildings and fields and trees as it surged towards the sea. 'Wait a minute,' he said, 'that river is more powerful, more important than me; look how it sweeps aside everything in its path – I wish I was a river!'

And suddenly there was a clap of thunder, and a sound just like a mighty fanfare on the biggest organ in the world, and he was a mighty river, rolling on relentlessly, never ending, towards the sea. Now I'm powerful, now I'm important; I'm a RIVER!'

But as the river approached the sea, a great rock stood directly in its way. The river couldn't go over it, or under it; the only way was to split and go round it. And the river thought, 'Wait a minute! This rock is more important, more powerful, and even stronger than me – I wish I was a rock!'

And suddenly there was a clap of thunder, and a sound just like a mighty fanfare on the biggest organ in the world, and he felt his whole body slowly solidifying, settling down, thickening, hardening, and finally he was a rock. The strongest, oldest rock in the world. And he thought, 'Now I'm powerful, now I'm important! Nothing can break me, nothing can change me; I'm a ROCK!'

For thousands of years he was content, strong and happy with his own importance. But then one day he felt a little itch on his shoulder. Looking down he saw a little quarryman with his hammer and chisel, scoring a line to make a cut to split off a lump of stone. The quarryman worked patiently, methodically. Now if he, and future generations of quarrymen keep on chipping away, they'll wear away that great rock as sure as hammers are hammers and chisels are chisels.

So you see, this story ended where it began – with the Portland quarryman. It shows that the quarrymen and the work they do is just as important as the king – some might say, more important; and, of course, that quarryman could just as well have been a nurse, a postman, a teacher – or even a storyteller!

Quarrying Portland stone has been a vital part of the island's character and economy for hundreds of years.

Roman coffins have been found made from Portland stone, and the material has been used in London since the fourteenth century, most notably in the Tower of London. Sir Christopher Wren chose Portland stone for his rebuilding of St Paul's Cathedral after the Great Fire of 1666, and the stone has been popular as a prized material for public buildings ever since. It is only very recently that the work has become less strenuous and labour intensive. Sophisticated machinery now does most of the work that was formerly done by hammer, plug and feathers, and explosives. It was highly skilled and dangerous work, based on years of practical experience with the materials involved, which allowed the quarrymen to get a good, straight split in the rock. A former quarryman now living in Bridport recalled that his first job, starting work in a Portland quarry at the age of fourteen, was to run a piece of lighted newspaper along a line laboriously chipped into the rock to take a row of wedges, before the main split was attempted. When he asked the purpose of the fire, he was told it was 'to keep them necromancers away'. Songs were used in the style of sea shanties – to allow the men to strike their sledgehammers on the wedges rhythmically.

Nowadays most of the stone is carried by road transport, but formerly the stone was lowered over the cliffs into barges using derricks, some of which can still be seen on the island.

8

MRS JEANS AND THE SOLDIERS

Now Susannah – that's Mrs Jeans you know – she lives opposite the alehouse here in Belchalwell, helps out from time to time. She don't think much of soldiers, and there's a good reason for that, and I'll tell 'ee all about it. Course, what with her son Sammy being a sailor, it was the senior service that always attracted her attention, and whenever the postman brought a letter from some foreign port – which wasn't often – she would be over to Ibberton to call on the schoolmistress. She'd get her to read it over for her, and find out on the globe where the port might be that the letter had come from. And on the rare occasions when the gallant sailor did return, Susannah was the proudest woman in the village, and the tales of her son's exploits kept her going for months afterwards.

Most sailors bring home parrots or ships in bottles, or shawls, don't they? But not Sammy; he brought a yucca plant from South America, and be blowed if it didn't flourish here in the village. To give Mrs Jeans her due, she never begrudged a cutting or shoot; so it wasn't long before all the gardens in the village began to take on a distinctly tropical flavour.

Anyway, soldiers was regarded as an inferior breed, so one afternoon, when a Sergeant of the 39th Foot and his men come marching through, and called in here to wet their whistles, you can be sure her curtains were twitching.

All this happened before I was born, but we don't have that much to talk about round here of a winter's night, so when something tremendous happens, the tale gets retold many times. I know it as well as if I'd been there myself. And for once, Granfer Ben wasn't in charge – he was powerless in the face of events as you might say!

This all happened after the Battle of Inkerman in the Crimean War – do 'ee remember? Sergeant Fleming and his men were on their way to Shaftesbury recruiting, and, having hauled over Bulbarrow, they took a wrong turning at the Cross, and ended up here in Bel, where Albert Philips was driving a herd of cows.

Albert – you all know Albert, don't you? Long, gawky lookin' fella with hair sticking out all over and his hat on one side of his head – cowman, see – not a pretty picture, unless you like the pictures in the *Police Gazette*! Well, Albert advised them to call in here and wet their whistles.

'Thank you my fine fellow,' says the sergeant – tall chap he was, with a fine moustache and a uniform to match – 'and might you be looking to leave behind the plough and take the King's shilling and serve your Queen and Country?'

Well, no one had ever called Albert a fine fellow before, but he was as wise inside as he looked stupid outside, so he said, 'Yes, Sergeant, thank you very much! And if you and your men would take over the cows, milk 'em twice a day and exchange your fine red coats for my old smock frock, and your muskets for this pitchfork, I'd be delighted to go!' Whereupon the sergeant turned pale, ordered the drummer to beat up 'Darby Kelly', and they marched on briskly into Bel – 'By the left, quick march!'

> My Grandsire beat the drum complete, his name was Darby Kelly Oh,
> No lad so true at rat tat too, at roll call or Reveille O,
> When Great Wolfe died his country's pride
> To Arms to Arms my father beat!
> Each hill and dale remembers still
> How long, how loud, how clear, how sweet!

It so happened that Granfer Ben was out in the fields at the time, so Grandmother Maria served them cider and managed to find some bread and cheese. Now, whether it was the cider got into their heads, or the walk across Bulbarrow in the sun, those soldiers began to get very relaxed! At last the sergeant announces that he's to marry a Sturminster girl in a month's time, and the reception should be nowhere but in Rose's Alehouse. Well, Gran was wondering what she'd got herself in to, so she says, 'Are you sure Sergeant? We don't have much to offer compared to girt places like Blandford and Stur.'

'Nonsense Mrs Rose,' says the Sergeant, 'we don't want anything fancy. My Kate's a Sturminster girl, she don't have no airs and graces. You can provide excellent bread and cheese I suppose?'

'Oh yes, sir,' says Gran, 'Lowbrook Farm cheese, and Blue Vinny.'

'Very fine, very fine,' says the Sergeant, licking his chops, 'and perhaps some ham or beef?'

'Oh yes sir, and a rabbit or two if the keeper's not … if they are obtainable sir.'

'Excellent,' remarked the soldier, 'and for dessert?'

'Dessert?' Gran was momentarily flummoxed, 'Oh, bless 'ee, you mean afters! Well, I suppose there's apple cake sir …'

'Apple cake? Prime!' cried the Sergeant, as Gran refilled his tankard.

'Yes sir, and the apples sir, be …'

'Yes, Mrs Rose?'

'They be Warriors sir; Dorset Warriors, just like yourselves!'

So that settled it. There would be a party of twenty, and the sergeant would pay 5s a head. So Gran wrote down the date on a piece of paper. Then she had her masterstroke, and even Robert Roberts had to allow it was as pretty a piece of brainwork as he'd ever heard, 'And will the bride and her maids be requiring gloves Sergeant?'

'Gloves, Mrs Rose?' says the Sergeant, scratching his head, 'it's the middle of the summer!'

'No sir, I mean embroidered wedding gloves,' Gran was beginning to enjoy herself, ''tis all the fashion round here, sir.'

'But where can they be had, ma'am?'

'Why, here sir. My daughters Lucy and Eliza will be pleased to supply them to 'ee!'

'Then gloves it shall be!' said the military man decisively, 'but Mrs Rose, what shall we do for music? You can't have a wedding without music.'

Gran then delivered the *coup de grâce*, 'My husband, Mr Benjamin Rose, will play for 'ee, sir; he be the best fiddler this side of Stur! You should hear him play "The Eagel"!'

So, when Granfer came home, it was to find that the biggest event ever known in the alehouse had been organised without his knowing. Gran went over the road and asked Mrs Jeans to make an apple cake for twenty, and Ben took out his handwritten book of country dances, and set about practising all his soldier tunes for the occasion. Their titles reflected fifty years of tumultuous campaigning in Europe: 'Blue and Buff', 'Waterloo', 'The Soldier's Fancy', 'Captain Flemings Delight', 'The Recov'ry', and 'Hessian Camp'.

Well, the great day came, and the wedding party arrived, the redcoats making an arch of crossed muskets as the sergeant and his blushing bride entered the alehouse. And by all accounts Gran and Mrs Jeans had done them proud; the place was spotless, floor swept, table scrubbed, greenery everywhere, and two barrels at the back ready broached, and over the fireplace a paper with the old regimental motto, *Primus in Indis*. And even Mrs Jeans had to allow that for the first two hours all went down as sweetly as apple pie and those soldiers were good as gold.

Well, then the *pièce de résistance* – the apple cake – came in.

Granfer told 'em that Mrs Jeans was famous for it; it was a recipe from her mother, and was so delicious that when old Granfer Jeans lay upstairs a-dying, and the boy went up to ask him what he might like, the old man said, 'You tell your mother I should like a last little bit of her apple cake.'

And he come down and told her and she said, 'No no, you go back up and tell him he can't have that; I want that for his funeral!'

Anyhow, by this time the soldiers were getting very merry, and Ben was beginning to feel uneasy as to how the evening was proceeding. But the sergeant called for more ale and cider and slapped down another guinea, and Granfer thought it best to humour them and get them to shake off the liquor with a dance or two.

By the time they'd finished their jigs and reels, it was getting on for midnight, and Ben says, 'You'll be anxious to be getting off for your honeymoon, Sergeant!'

The sergeant rose shakily to his feet, called for brandy, and rather unsteadily raised a toast to the bride:

> Kate, my dear,
> May your glasses always be full!
> May the roof over your head always be strong
> And may you be in Heaven half an hour
> Before the devil knows you're dead. Hip Hip Hip Hooray!

But then, blowed if they didn't all sit down again and pick up their mugs, and Granfer, fearing they might never leave, said something he regretted for the rest of his life. But it was quite understandable, it was done to get them out, 'Why don't 'ee step outside and fire a volley on yer muskets to salute the bride and groom as they leave?'

Well, the soldiers allowed that this was the best idea yet, and they all cheered and scrambled for their muskets, and the sergeant thanked all concerned, shook Gran by the hand and even kissed Mrs Jeans on both cheeks. He then called on Granfer to play 'Waterloo', and the soldiers and their sweethearts trooped unsteadily outside.

Then the sergeant lined up his men and called them to order:

> Prime and Load! Handle Cartridge! Prime! About! Draw Ram
> Rods! Ram Down the Cartridge! Present! FIRE!!!!

On the command fire, there was the most tre-mend-ous explosion ever heard in Bel. It sent the rooks fleeing from the elm trees, and a great shower of sparks and smoke rolling down the street. The soldiers and their women went off down the lane, and Granfer and the rest retired thankfully to bed, until ...

Fire! Fire! FIRE!

Thinking it was the soldiers come back they ran out, but no, the wadding from the muskets had landed in the thatch opposite, and Mrs Jeans' roof was well ablaze. Oh, they did what they could; some ran to the brook with pails for water, some tried to pull the thatch off with rakes and pitchforks, and Granfer sent Robert up Dark Lane to Okeford to call for the famous fire engine. Of course, it took a while for the firemen to find their helmets, and then the horse had to be harnessed and the engine pulled out; but pretty soon they were dashing up the lane with the bell a-ringing. But by the time they arrived, all that was left was a row of smouldering walls, burnt rafters, heaps of sodden thatch, and Mrs Jeans' furniture under a rick cover in the middle of the road. What a sight! Well, 'twas the talk of the place for months afterwards, and it even got into the *Western Gazette*, although they got most of the details wrong. But back then folk were resilient and used to misfortunes. If something went wrong you just got on and put it to rights. Mrs Jeans moved to another cottage, and after a while she could even laugh at what had happened. And as she said, 'Well, what can you expect of soldiers? If they'd been sailors, they'd have had plenty of water to put out the fire!'

Benjamin Rose (1796–1877) was a farmer, alehouse keeper and fiddle player in the tiny hamlet of Belchalwell, which lies just north of Bulbarrow Hill in the Blackmore Vale area of Dorset. In 1820 Ben sat down in the alehouse to write out his repertoire of country dance tunes, and all the melodies mentioned in this tale can be found in the book. The Dorset Warrior in the story refers not just to Sergeant Fleming's men, but also to a favourite local variety of apple still to be found growing in the area. Gloving and button making (doing buttony) were local cottage industries. The famous fire engine at Okeford Fitzpaine can still be seen, displayed in the centre of the village. In 1852 the *Western Gazette* contained a brief report of the fire:

> On Wednesday last a fire, attended with great loss of property, broke out on the premises of a Mr Rose of Belchalwell. A salute of firearms was given in honour of a wedding party who had adjourned to Mr Rose's beer-house and some ignited wadding fell on the thatched roof. The fire extended to four cottages on the opposite side of the road, which were reduced to ruins.

9

THE FOX AND THE KEYS

Good morning! Do come in. Don't mind me; I'm just doing the flowers for Sunday. Take as long as you like, I'll close up when you've finished. We try to keep the church open for as long as we can, but you do have to be so careful these days, don't you? They're lovely, aren't they, these old churches? The oldest buildings still standing in Dorset, and so much history in them. I love to feel a part of that. All those generations of people in here, altogether, singing their hymns, saying their prayers – the heart of the villages, aren't they? The guidebooks are over there, next to the postcards and the parish magazine.

When Harry – that's my husband – was alive, we were great bell-ringers and used to go all over Dorset, ringing the bells; it's a wonderful way to get to know the county, don't you think? And some of the old legends associated with the churches, well, they really get you thinking. Wimborne Minster – there was a whole abbey there at one time; the Vikings came up the Stour Valley and burnt the church to the ground. Three hundred years of compassion, devotion and nurture gone up in smoke. That curious little tower on the side of the minster was all that was left, that and a broken cross, and the old chest. It was a miracle it survived.

It has six locks, you know – the story is that it's one for each
of the six days of the week when God created the world;
what a treasure – and later on it contained relics, and was
an object of pilgrimage. Such a deep faith, to travel on foot
many miles to worship scraps of hair and bone that were
almost certainly fakes! You wouldn't find many people to
do it now, would you?

But the stories I love best about Wimborne are about
the nuns. They weren't always perfect, you know. They are
fallible, just like the rest of us; it makes them seem more
human somehow. One of the prioresses was very harsh
towards her nuns. She treated them very badly and, when
she died and was buried in the abbey graveyard, the nuns
crept out from their dormitory and danced on her grave
in the moonlight, to prevent her soul from ascending to
Heaven.

And then there's the story of the old portress who looked
after the inner gates and the abbey church – she locked it
up at night. She was always forgetting things. I can relate
to that! One night, after locking the church, she misplaced
the keys. The next day, they were nowhere to be found,
and, of course, the nuns couldn't get into the church to
worship. The prioress called them all together, and they
stood together in a circle outside the abbey and prayed
for the return of the keys so that they could re-enter their
church. On their way back, they were astonished to find a
dead fox with the keys in its mouth. Did the fox find them,
and like a magpie, want to take them? And was she struck
dead by prayer? Or did a thief take them, and, being struck
with remorse, decide to plant them on the fox? It's so long
ago, we will never know.

I expect you know the Cross on Batcombe Down? There's
a beautiful story of the priest who was summoned late one

stormy night to give the last rites to a dying parishioner.
He struggled across the down in the wind and rain, but as
he arrived at the woman's cottage he realised that he had
dropped the pyx that contained the consecrated Host somewhere. There was nothing for it but to retrace his steps and
try to find it, which you would think would be an impossible task. But when he climbed the hill, he was amazed
to see a shaft of fire reaching down from Heaven to earth.
As he came closer he saw all the sheep and cattle gathered in
a circle, kneeling around the pyx, and he was able to recover
it and complete his ministry. The cross up there is supposed
to mark the spot. Thomas Hardy wrote a poem about it.
Do you know it?

Then there's St Catherine's Chapel at Abbotsbury. You
get a wonderful view of it coming down the hill along the

coast road from Burton Bradstock. I'm told it's an even better landmark from sea, though I've never seen it from that angle myself. Did you know that you can go there to make a wish?

> A husband St Catherine
> A handsome one, St Catherine;
> A rich one, St Catherine;
> A nice one, St Catherine;
> And soon, St Catherine!

And there are 'wishing holes' in the stones; one for your knee and two smaller ones above for your hands.

Some of our oldest churches still have a West Gallery. That was where the musicians and singers used to be, before the Victorians altered so many churches and put organs into them. There's still one at Puddletown – you really should make time to stop and see it; and there was a gallery at West Lulworth years ago. One Christmas the singers and the musicians couldn't agree which carol to sing on Christmas morning. There was a fierce argument in the gallery at choir practice, but as there were more singers than musicians, the singers had their way. On Christmas morning, however, all the musicians were sat in the body of the church, arms folded, as much as to say, 'Go on then, do it without us.'

But the choir took it in their stride: 'Sal,' says the leader, 'pitch it for us!' And Sal, who had a beautiful clear soprano voice, did just that, and away they went. They chose, 'There Were Shepherds Abiding'– one of their own carols – and sang it right through to the end with never a hitch. The musicians went out of church with their tails between their legs, and they were mighty glad to creep back up to the gallery again once they had swallowed their pride.

Mind you, being bell-ringers, we used to get to see parts of the churches where most people never go; up rickety little ladders quite often, or twisty, dusty little stone steps (always carry a torch!), and then into the ringing chamber, which would often have the rules of the belfry written up on the walls. Then there'd be another ladder up beyond, past the bells to the roof of the tower, and sometimes we'd be allowed to get right up onto the roof itself, and then you see a sight to take your breath away – the whole town or village, and the countryside stretching away in all directions; exhilarating! And quite often, if you look down on the lead that lines the roof, you see the shapes of hands and boots, when people in the past have stood in the same spot, and looked at the same views, and drawn round their boot or hand, and carved their initials and the date into the lead.

Oh, I must tell you one other little story, before you look round, from St Peter's in Dorchester – you must visit that one! Apparently, on Christmas Eve in 1814, the clerk and the sexton were in the church, decorating it for Christmas morning. They hung a large bunch of mistletoe up over the Mayor's pew, polished up the brasses, and put fresh candles around the pulpit. They'd locked themselves in, so that Christmas Eve revellers couldn't burst in and disrupt their work in an unseemly way. When they had finished, it was late and very cold. They retired to the vestry to warm up, and somehow the idea entered their heads that a little sup of Communion wine to restore them wouldn't go amiss! They uncorked the bottle and took a little swig, and right at that moment the ghost of their late rector, Revd Nathaniel Templeman, rose up before them, glared at them, and shook his head angrily.

Well, as you can imagine, they were dumbstruck. The ghost rose up before them, still admonishing them, floated down the north aisle, and sank into the floor. The clerk fainted, and the sexton tried his best to say the Lord's Prayer. They were so troubled by what they'd seen that they told their friends and neighbours what they had done. They stuck to the tale, and said they were sure it was their old master, even though he was dead and gone, because he was wearing the same clothes and looking just as he did when he was alive.

Well, there, I've kept you far too long. If you'd sign the visitors' book when you've finished, that would lovely; and the postcards are 20p each, just put the money in the box in the wall.

10

COLONEL BROADREPP'S TALE

In my capacity as magistrate in the Beaminster area of west Dorsetshire, I have had occasion to listen to many tales of suffering, villainy and pitiful behaviour, so that one is apt to become inured to the infinite capacity for folly that exists in one's fellow creatures. Of course, my professional integrity prevents me from naming names in the many curious, tragic and occasionally comic cases that come before me; but since the story I am about to relate to you has appeared, albeit rather inaccurately, in no less a journal than the *Gentleman's Magazine*, I feel at liberty to comment on what was one of the most singular incidents ever brought before the bench.

In July of 1728 our local schoolmaster came to me with the vicar in a state of some agitation. Both of these gentlemen were well known to me as pillars of our little community, attending to both the spiritual and the practical needs of the younger generation in the town. I would not expect either of them to be easily misled by childish stories, or fall victim to juvenile pranks; indeed, Mr Collins the schoolmaster was justly feared for his sharpness, and supreme in the art of identifying and punishing liars and cheats.

The story that both men told me was that on the previous Saturday, 27 June, after school had finished and Mr Collins had dismissed his pupils, he left them to lock up the door to the schoolroom, not expecting to hear any more from them until the following Monday. It will be remembered by older inhabitants of Beaminster that the school was then held in the West Gallery of St Mary's Church, by kind permission of the vicar and churchwardens. When I queried his leaving the key with the boys, he replied that this was the usual practice; they were expected, quite rightly, to clear away their books, sweep the floors, refill the ink wells and sharpen the pens in readiness for the following week's work. The key was then returned by one of their number to the parish clerk.

It seems that a dozen of the scholars were playing ball in the churchyard before commencing their cleaning duties – something that, while not entirely approved of by the vicar, is nonetheless tolerated on the grounds that it is better for boys to let off steam in an innocent and healthful activity rather than get into worse mischief on their way home. While this game was in progress, four of the lads went up into the gallery to commence their janitorial duties, and they were startled to hear a noise from inside the main body of the church below, which they described as being rather like the sound one might produce by beating a large brass pan. They ran out to tell their comrades, and came to the conclusion that someone was hiding in the church playing a game with them, trying to scare them. A few minutes later, however, they heard a second noise, and, running right round the church, they came to the belfry door and heard what they described as someone preaching, and the sound of psalms being sung. This, of course, was on a Saturday, when such a thing was not to be expected;

but they did not dare to look in, or think to investigate, and instead, with the thoughtlessness of youth, they went back to their football game.

Shortly after this, one of the lads went up the gallery steps to collect his schoolbook, and was startled to see a small coffin lying on one of the school benches, about six feet from the door. He immediately called back to his fellows to come and see, and they attempted to crowd in through the schoolroom door. Five of the twelve then witnessed the following extraordinary sight: the apparition of a boy of about their own age called John Daniel, a schoolfellow who had died seven weeks previously. He was sitting calmly in his place, reading a book. At this point I interrupted Mr Collins to ask why it should be that only five of the boys saw the apparition. He replied that the gallery steps were narrow and the doorway was low and that, although all twelve were able to see the coffin, only those boys quickest up the steps were able to look into the length of the schoolroom and see the apparition at the far end near the master's desk.

At first they were uncertain as to the identity of the ghost, until Daniel's half-brother cried out, 'There sits our John with such a coat on as I have.' Mr Collins was able to confirm to me that it was customary for the two boys to be clad in identical coats, obtained from Mr Stainer's tailoring establishment in the town. Then the other boys, who could not see, demanded to know what the apparition was doing, and were told that he was sitting, pen in hand, intent on his studies. They all watched in awe for some minutes until one Johnson, a weak-minded boy much given to silly behaviour, suggested they throw a stone at him (Mr Collins had often, to his sorrow as he put it, been obliged to punish the lad for stone-throwing and other inappropriate behaviour,

as the school punishment book well attests). The other schol-
ars tried to prevent this rash action, but Johnson cried out,
'Take it!' and flung the stone, and the apparition of John
Daniel disappeared.

I must admit I was somewhat perplexed. Both men were
obviously convinced by the veracity of the boys' story, and we
were all puzzled as how best to proceed. In the end, despite
their youth, it was decided that the correct approach was
to be perfectly practical about the matter, and for myself to
examine them individually to discover the truth of their story.
It will be appreciated that of course all kinds of wild and
exaggerated stories had immediately spread around the town
and the countryside beyond. The people at that time were
very susceptible to anything of a supernatural nature; the
youth of the apparition, and the fact that the event took
place in broad daylight, only adding to the mystery and
excitement surrounding the case.

I therefore summoned the boys one by one to my
library, and examined them as to what they had seen.
Despite my scepticism, I found myself increasingly
convinced that they had indeed seen an apparition resem-
bling their former schoolmate. All were able to describe
accurately the coffin, including the decoration on the
hinges, even though none of them had been allowed to
attend the funeral. Of course, it is entirely possible that
they had been talking of their former schoolfellow – his
death had only occurred seven weeks before, and naturally many of his possessions were still in the schoolroom
– and that some sort of group hysteria had caused them
to imagine that they saw him. Such a rational explanation
was rather deflated, however, by a very strong statement
from a twelve-year-old lad who had recently moved from
Bridport into Beaminster, who did not attend Mr Collins'

school until after the death of John Daniel, and could not have known John Daniel. This observant lad, who I will call William J., not only accurately described the boy, so that there could be no doubt that he had seen him, but he also noticed that Daniel wore a white bandage of rag, bound on one of his hands.

I next determined to examine the lady who laid out John Daniel for interment, and she confirmed to me on oath that the boy had been lame in his right hand, and wore a bandage on it, which she had removed from him in her preparations before he was placed in the coffin.

The boy had been found dead in a field outside the town and had been buried without an inquest because his mother had said that he was subject to fits, and this was naturally assumed to be the cause of death. It seemed to me, however, that the only way to settle the matter was to order the exhumation of the body. With the vicar's approval this sad task was duly done, all the proper niceties being observed, and the corpse, which was not much decayed, was examined by Mr Breakspear, a self-styled chirurgeon from Bridport – Dr Pottinger being himself indisposed and unable, much to my regret, to attend to the matter.

A coroner's inquest was held; the verdict reached being that the boy had most probably been strangled. The evidence for this was that two women 'of good repute' who had seen the body before it was interred came forward to say that they had noticed a black mark or 'list' around the boy's neck. The joiner who made the coffin attested that he had also seen this mark, since the boy had not been shrouded in the normal way, but instead was merely laid in the coffin with a piece of cloth below him and another on top. However, the crucial piece of evidence, that the boy's neck was dislocated, was not obtained, since Mr Breakspear found himself unable to state categorically that this was the case – we may imagine that Dr Pottinger would not have been so lax in his examination, or feeble in his diagnosis!

Altogether a singular and disturbing case, unsatisfactory in that no one was ever brought to justice for the supposed murder of poor John Daniel. But it may be that the notoriety of the incident, and the thoroughness of the investigation that followed, for which I suppose I can claim some credit, was in some way sufficient to allow the bones of the unfortunate youngster to rest in peace.

11

LITTLE DICKY MILBURN

Well, one morning Dicky came into the house and his wife said, 'Dicky, oh Dicky, I'm taken terrible bad with the colic; go into Charmouth and get me a bottle of whisky. I reckon I shall die if you don't. Hurry along, there's a good man!'

Well, Dicky was no doctor, but he thought it was strange to think about curing the colic with whisky, and he said as much to his wife; but she insisted it was the only thing that would do the trick, and then she says, 'Come to think of it, you'd better go on into Lyme to get some decent stuff, because that whisky they sell in Charmouth is no good. And hurry, I reckon I shall die if you don't.'

Well, Lyme was quite a lot further, and Dicky had already been out two hours milking the cows, so he was reluctant to go. But his wife kept on moaning and groaning about the whisky, so in the end, for the sake of some peace and quiet, he set off down the road to Lyme.

He'd only got about halfway when he met Tom the carter, on his way to Palmers Brewery in Bridport with a load of hops. 'Morning, Dicky,' said Tom brightly, 'and how are you this fine day?'

'I'm all right,' said Dicky, 'but Susan isn't. No, her's taken terrible bad, and her reckons her'll die, and the only thing that'll cure it is a bottle of whisky, and I've got to go to Lyme to get the right stuff.'

'Die, be blowed!' said Tom briskly. 'That wife of yours is as fit as a fiddle. I'll tell you what it is, Dicky, she's in league with the parson, and she just wants you out of the way for a couple of hours!'

Well, Dicky said he couldn't and wouldn't believe such a thing of his Susan. So Tom says, 'Alright then, Dicky, I'll tell you what: you get into one of these here empty hop sacks of mine, and we'll go past your place, and we'll find out the truth of it; and if I'm wrong, I'll buy you two bottles of whisky!'

That seemed like a good offer, so Dicky clambered into the hop sack, taking a stick with him, and Tom tied up the neck. Then off they went in the wagon until they got to Dicky's house. Tom stopped the wagon and hammered on the door with his horse-whip. Out came Mrs Milburn looking flushed, smoothing down her clothes.

'Oh, Tom!' she says, 'Well! This is a surprise! What can I do for you?'

'I've had a misfortune, Mrs Milburn,' said Tom, 'I was going over the ford a way back, and the horse slipped, and one of my hop sacks fell in the water. Can I bring it in and dry it out by your fire?'

'Oh, well, yes, I suppose so,' said Mrs Milburn. 'I … I've got the parson here at the moment, on Church business you know, but I'm sure he won't mind …'

'Always happy to talk to the parson,' says Tom cheerfully; and with that he jumps down, lugs in the sack, with Dicky inside, and sets it down by the fire. Right opposite sat the parson in his stockinged feet, looking very much at home, with a large tankard of beer in his hand, his collar undone and his best riding boots warming by the fire.

'Ah, good morning Thomas,' says the parson, 'and how are you this morning? I haven't seen you in church recently!'

'No sir,' said Tom, 'and I'm surprised to see you out visiting your flock at this time of day.'

'I am always available to tend to the spiritual needs of my parishioners,' said the parson loftily.

Mrs Milburn fetched a small glass of ale for Tom, and they all sat by the fire.

'Well, Thomas, I hear you are a bit of a singer,' remarked the parson. 'I've often heard you singing away on that wagon of yours. How about giving us a song while we wait for your hops to dry?'

'Willingly,' says Tom, 'but gentlemen first, I'm sure. You begin, sir.'

The parson needed no second bidding. This is what he sang:

Oh Dicky, oh Dicky, how little dost thou think

I'm here eating thy meat and drinking thy drink!

If God spare my life, I'll lie with thy wife,

And oh, for a tankard of ale, of more ale,

Ale, of more ale,

O for a tankard of ale, of more ale.

Then Mrs Milburn chimed in, and she began to sing, and her song went like this:

Oh Dicky, oh Dicky, since thou art from home,
God send thee fair journey, and long may you roam.
If ever I do lack, I've a priest at my back,
And oh, for a tankard of ale of more ale,
Ale, of more ale,
O for a tankard of ale, of more ale.

Then Tom cleared his throat, and sang out bravely:

Oh Dicky, oh Dicky, since thou art so near,
Then out from my hop sack thy head shall appear;
If a friend thou dost lack, I'll stand at thy back,
And oh, for a tankard of ale, of more ale,
Ale, of more ale,
O for a tankard of ale, of more ale.

The sack flew open and Dicky appeared with a great cry, waving the stick. Well, the parson was out of that chair and off down the road before you could say Jack Robinson. He ran off so fast, he forgot his best riding boots, and never had the nerve to come back for them. Well, of course, Mrs Milburn begged Dicky to forgive her, and promised she'd never do the like again. Dicky, he didn't say anything. He just sat down, reached over for the boots and pulled them on. They fitted perfectly. 'Well that's good,' he remarked. 'Parson looked after your spiritual needs, and now he's looked after my soles!' And Dicky wore those boots to church the next Sunday, and parson didn't dare say a word!

And we'll send to the Tap for more ale, for more ale,

Ale, for more ale,

O we'll send to the tap for more ale, for more ale.

Cante-fables such as this are rare in Dorset. This one was collected by Robert and Henry Hammond from Farmer William Miller in Wootton Fitzpaine in April 1906. A note on the manuscript states that the story was well known in Somerset and Oxfordshire. The end is often more brutal:

He banished his wife the very same day,

Gelded the parson and sent him away!

12

BILLY GRAY'S GANG

Well, it was the schoolmaster who started it. Turkey Hawkins he was called, on account of how he went bright red from the neck upwards whenever he was cross or flustered. Turkey told us last thing one September afternoon that the following day we must all write an essay on 'Adventures after School', and we all scratched our heads as to how to begin, for as far as we knew, there wouldn't be any. Our village was a quiet sort of place, tucked away below the Ridgeway, where nothing much happened – leastways, nothing we could tell him about!

Any rate, after school and a bit of tea we all met up as usual.

'What shall us play tonight? Hare and Hounds?'

That was the big favourite, a kind of hide-and-seek that took us all through the village and up the lane onto the hills and the Ridgeway. Mary set off and we shielded our eyes and counted to 100, then began to sing out:

HOLLER FOLLER! HOLLER FOLLER!

From way up the lane, out of the gathering gloom, came FOLLER! And off we went. At it for an hour or so we were, until the game led us past Farmer Diment's orchard. We all leaned over the wall. The trees were heavy with apples, just asking to be picked. 'Do we dare?' we thought. We knew if the old man caught us in his orchard he'd come after us on his horse, Champion, and one or two had felt the sharp end of his stick more than once. But Diment's apples were the best in the village, so a couple went over the wall, and it wasn't long before they came back with a bag, and a hat, full of apples. Just as we were going down the lane we heard a horse and an angry cry, and we didn't stop to find out who it was – we knew! Off we went again, full pelt; most of us headed back up towards the Ridgeway, but Bill and Jack went the other way, until they came to the churchyard. They looked in, and over in the corner by the big yew there was a freshly dug grave.

'Ah,' said Billy, 'that's the place. We'll get down in there and share out the apples.' So in they went through the gate, but as they did Jack dropped a couple of Diment's apples, but he didn't dare to stop and pick 'em up, for they could hear the farmer coming along the lane on Champion, cursing at the top of his voice.

Well Bill and Jack got safe into the grave and began to share out the apples in the old traditional way, 'One for me, and one for thee, two for me and two for thee, one for me, one for thee, two for me, two for thee …'

Now, while all this was happening, the village policeman was on his rounds. There had been a lot of trouble locally with thieves stealing things from churches, so he was very careful to check the church. He shone his torch all round, but couldn't see anything; but he heard something, so he listened intently, and he heard, 'One for me, and one for thee, two for me and two for thee, one for me, one for thee, two for me, two for thee …'

Well, that policeman jumped on his bike, pedalled straight down to the police station, and burst in through the door, calling out, 'Sergeant, Sergeant, come quick!

God and the Devil are in the churchyard, sharing out the souls of the dear departed; come quick!'

So the sergeant got on his bike, and together the two of them pedalled back up the hill to the church and stood by the gate, not noticing Farmer Diment's two rosy apples by the gatepost. And they shone their torches, and couldn't see anything; but they heard, 'One for me, and one for thee, two for me and two for thee, one for me, one for thee, two for me, two for thee and that's all!'

'That's all?' said the other voice, from deep inside the grave, 'what about those two we left by the gate?'

Well, those two policemen were off down the road as fast as they could pedal. But after a bit they slowed down, thought a bit. Then one says to the other, 'Are you thinking what I'm thinking Constable?'

'I might be sir; what are you thinking?'

'I don't reckon that was God and the Devil at all – I reckon that was those village kids up to their games again!'

'You could be right Sarg; what shall we do?'

'Do, Constable? Why, you follow 'em on your bike, and I'll go back to the station and await your report. Get on with it!'

So the policeman got wearily on his bicycle and pedalled back up the lane. Meanwhile, we'd all met up, and the next thing was, 'What about Gunner and Charlie?'

Well, these two old chaps were neighbours up in Church Lane, but they didn't get on, always rowing they were. So one of us crept up with a piece of string and tied their door handles together, knocked on both doors and ran off. Well, there was an almighty row, and then they looked down the lane and saw us, so we legged it. But Gunner and Charlie came after us, nearly knocked over the policeman on his bike, so he joined in the chase, all of 'em shouting out: 'Stop, Stop, STOP!'

We headed up towards the Ridgeway and began to sing:

RUN, RUN, AS FAST AS YOU CAN,
YOU CAN'T CATCH US WE'RE BILLY GRAY'S GANG!

Up the lane was the village hall, and it was Women's Institute night, and we stopped to peer in through the window, and there was all the village ladies listening carefully to a lady in a great hat, talking away and waving her arms she was. And Bill said, 'Let's put a bag over the chimbley like we did a fortnight ago.'

But the others said no, the ladies were wise to that,;besides, there was no fire in the fireplace so 'twas no good. Then Mary said, 'What about Nazareth?'

Nazareth was the donkey, kept in the field by the wood; and with the aid of a couple of Diment's apples we got him out and down to the hall. Someone opened the door, smacked the donkey's bum and in he went, hee-hawing away – glorious confusion! Well we legged it again, and it didn't take those women long to get the donkey out and chase after us, so now there was Nazareth and the Women's Institute ladies, and Gunner and Charlie, and the policeman on his bike all puffing and panting and crying out: 'Stop, Stop, STOP!'

Again we sung out:

RUN, RUN, AS FAST AS YOU CAN,
YOU CAN'T CATCH US WE'RE BILLY GRAY'S GANG!

But we decided discretion was the better part of valour, and ran right over the Ridgeway until we could see the sea, and down the other side till we nearly reached the Crown.

Suddenly we stopped, arrested in our tracks by a blue light – had the police sent to Dorchester for reinforcements? But no, the blue light wasn't on the road, it was out at sea, and there were people down on the beach, landing something. Then, in the darkness, we heard the tramping of heavy feet and a low hum of voices:

In South Australia I was born, heave away, haul away,
South Australia round Cape Horn, we're bound for South Australia

We were pressed into the bushes beside the track, scarcely daring to blink, and they came past us so close that we could see the whites of their eyes and the casks slung round their necks, and the leader, a tall man in a big-brimmed hat, anxiously looking around him all the time, 'Steady there lads. Aye, aye Emmanuel. Keep them tubs moving; quickly now.'

Suddenly we were grabbed by strong hands. 'What the Devil are ye doing here?'

'Are they Revenue?'

'No. Kids, Mr Charles, spying on us!'

Then Bill suddenly turned and bit the hand of the chap who was holding him. He cursed, fell over the tubs he was carrying, and somehow the rest of us broke free, and hared off back up the Ridgeway, and we didn't stop until we reached the gorse up on the top, and crept along under the shelter of a hedge in the moonlight. And somewhere behind us in the dark were Emmanuel, Charles and the smugglers, Nazareth the donkey, the Women's Institute, Gunner and Charlie, and the policeman on his bicycle, all calling out faintly in the distance: 'Stop, Stop, STOP!'

Well, we hardly dared to breathe, so we just whispered:

RUN, RUN, AS FAST AS YOU CAN,
YOU CAN'T CATCH US WE'RE BILLY GRAY'S GANG!

After a bit we climbed on, until we came to some shadowy shapes standing up from the gorse and the grass; great
mounds, black against the night sky.

'Where are we?' said Mary.

'Bincombe Bumps, of course,' said Bill. 'We'll hide here, and
get our breath back.' So we huddled down in the darkness in
amongst the barrows. Strange, eerie places they are at night, I
can tell you. Turkey reckons they're the graves of old warriors.
Some say there's treasure in 'em, and we always look in the mole-
hills and rabbit burrows in the hope of finding some, but we
never have. As we lay in the grass, with the whole of Weymouth
Bay below us and the lights of Portland gleaming in the distance,
we began to hear a murmur, then a whisper, then the beginnings
of a tune, and then music; humming music coming at first from
one barrow, then two, then all of them. It properly spooked us
it did, so we legged it again, away from the singing bumps and
heading full pelt along the Ridgeway until, right in front of us,
we saw a big, stout chap on a horse. At first we thought it was
Farmer Diment caught up with us, but no, it wasn't Champion,
this horse was completely white – and so was the rider.

'Hello there!' he calls out. 'What are you children doing
out so late, eh? Tell me that, eh, what, what?'

'Out playing games, sir. We got lost – got to get home.'

'Then jump up on my horse, I'm going your way, what,
what! Always happy to go to Weymouth!'

And somehow we all managed to climb on the back of
the horse, the whole gang, with Bill hanging on to the rider's
waist, though his arms would scarcely reach around. The rider
dug his spurs in and away we went, at top speed. We went all
along the top of the Ridgeway in the moonlight, all of us, with
the sea to the left of us and the lights of Dorchester away in the
distance on the right. The horse went full pelt – trot, canter,
gallop – and the strange thing was that her hooves made no

sound at all on the turf. All we could hear was the sound of
the wind. And when we turned round we could just make
out the singing barrows, and behind them the smugglers, and
Nazareth the donkey, and the Women's Institute, Gunner and
Charlie, and the policeman on his bicycle, all shaking their
fists in our direction, but there was nothing they could do.

'Whoa!' We stopped all of a sudden. In front of us, standing tall, barring the way, was a strong figure in a cocked hat
and greatcoat, with a telescope under his arm.

'We can't go any further my dears,' said our horseman,
'that's Old Admiral Hardy. We can't get past. He stopped the
whole French Navy at Trafalgar! I'm afraid we're no match
for him, what, what! There's your way home. Goodnight!'

And with that, he turned the horse about and galloped off
in the direction of Osmington, leaving us to pick our way
down the hill and back to our various homes.

'Listen,' said Bill, before we parted, 'don't say a word; all agreed?'

'Agreed!'

'And when we gets to school tomorrow, this is what we'll write …' and we all went into a huddle as Bill whispered in our ears.

So the next day at school, Turkey sets us all the essay, gives us half an hour to write it, and at the end of the half hour, he calls in the papers. We'd all written, 'Last night I had no adventures at all, because I had to stay in to do my homework.'

Well, Turkey went bright red even by his own standards, but he knew when he was beaten, so he made us sing instead, the Old White Horse song:

> The old white horse wants setting to rights
> And the squire has promised good cheer
> So we'll give him a scrape to keep him in shape
> And he'll last for many's a year

Some of the anecdotes and short stories contained in Billy Gray's Gang come from the villages below the Ridgeway west and east of Weymouth, and were collected as part of an oral history project for Dorset Area of Outstanding Natural Beauty in 2010/11. Other elements, including the reminiscence of playing Hare and Hounds, come from Dorothy Coombes of Portesham. The two great man-made landmarks on the Ridgeway are the Osmington White Horse – carved on the hillside in 1808 – and Hardy's Monument, the memorial to Nelson's Captain, Thomas Masterman Hardy, which overlooks his native village of Portesham. The tower is said to resemble a telescope.

13

THE OLD KING
OF CORFE

Now this wasn't in your time, it wasn't in my time – this was in the time when Purbeck quarrymen maintained their rights of way to Ower Quay by kicking a football, and birds built their nests in old men's beards.

There was an old fisherman who lived in Swanage. One day he sailed out into the bay and cast his nets and waited. After a while the corks began to bob, and he knew that a shoal of fish had swum into his net, so he hauled it in. Amongst the fish and the seaweed and the shells was a box, about the size of a shoe-box, and when he opened the box there was a baby boy inside – and he was alive. The fisherman took off his jumper to wrap up the little boy, and he quickly set sail for the shore, taking the child back to his wife. The fisherman's wife was delighted with the baby because they had no children of their own. Together they raised the boy to the best of their ability, and taught him all the practical things they knew. The fisherman's wife taught him to cook and sew, to keep a house and to tend the garden; and the old man passed on to him all the skills of the sea: how to tell the tide and the weather, how to bait a line and mend a net, and where and when to go fishing and sell a catch. But there were two things that neither of them could teach the growing boy: how to read and how to write. Neither the fisherman nor his wife had ever learned those skills themselves, although they had both managed to get by. Still, more than anything else, they wanted their son to be able to read and write.

Well one day, when the boy was about ten years old, he and his adoptive father were sat outside the cottage mending nets ready for that night's fishing. On the road coming towards them were three figures. When they got closer they could see that one of the figures was a tall man wearing a crown, and that the other two looked a lot like him. They were juggling three coloured balls each, which were about the size of the footballs that the quarrymen of Corfe kick through the village once a year to establish their ancient quarry rights.

Then the tall man spoke and he said, 'I am the Old King of Corfe Castle, and these are my two sons. If you will let me take your son for one year, I will teach him to read and write, and turn him into the cleverest boy in Dorset.'

The fisherman was mesmerised by the coloured balls as they looped and twisted in the air, and he thought, 'Well, I can't teach him myself, and if he can't read or write there'll be nothing for him but to live the same life that I have lived, and toil day and night in the cold seas for a bare living, and Lord knows, the fishing is not what it was …' So in the end he agreed, and the King and his two sons took the boy and off they went down the road towards Corfe.

Just then out came the fisherman's wife and she asked where the boy was, and when the fisherman told her about the King and his promise she cried and said, 'Oh God help us, what have you done? I'll never see my dear son again!'

But she was wrong, because a year to the day, as the old fisherman sat mending his nets, four figures came walking up the road towards him. When they got closer, he was delighted to see that it was the Old King of Corfe and his two sons, each juggling three coloured balls, and in front was his own son, proudly juggling seven coloured balls; they twisted and spun in the air until the fisherman was dizzy with excitement and joy. He called his wife and she came running out and flung her arms around the boy, and at that moment there was no happier family in the whole of the Isle of Purbeck.

Then the King said to the fisherman, 'Your son is now the cleverest boy in Dorset; he can read and write. He's the best pupil I've ever had. In fact, he's so good that I have a proposition for you: if you will let me take him for one more year, I can turn him into the cleverest boy in the whole country.'

Well, this time there was no hesitation; the fisherman and his wife both agreed that for the boy's sake he should go with the King; and the King promised to bring him back in a year's time.

A year later to the day, the fisherman and his wife sat outside the cottage on the old wooden bench, looking down the road towards Corfe, and nothing happened. There was no cloud of dust, no figures on the road, no king and boys, and no son, and they waited all day and night with sinking hearts. At last, when there was no sign of anyone, the old fisherman turned to his wife and said, 'It's my fault; I lost him, and now I'll find him.' He went indoors, took a bag, filled it with food and drink, and set off to find his son.

For weeks he walked all over Dorset. He went west into Somerset and Devon, and even took his life into his hands by crossing the Tamar, and everywhere he went, he asked the locals, 'Have you seen the Old King of Corfe and his two sons, juggling three coloured balls, and a young boy with them juggling seven coloured balls?'

The people looked at him as if he was mazed, and said they'd never seen such a sight, and that he should try the circus at Bodmin, or the carnival at Bridgwater.

And then as autumn came, and the weather began to close in, he came up over Exmoor and through Bristol into

Wiltshire, and still it was the same response to his question: 'No, I've never seen anyone like that round here.' But still the old fisherman didn't despair, and kept walking.

At last he came to the edge of the Cranborne Chase, that great forest set up by King John for his hunting and sports. On the edge of the forest he saw a charcoal fire burning, tended by a small old man, and the fisherman asked the same question, 'Have you seen the Old King of Corfe and his two sons, juggling three coloured balls, and a young boy with them juggling seven coloured balls?'

And the charcoal burner said, 'Well, no, not me; but if you take that track there through the hazel coppice and turn right when you reach the oaks beyond, there you'll see a keeper's cottage, and that's where my brother lives. He knows everything there is to be known about these woods, so he may be able to help you.'

The fisherman thanked him and made his way into the woods until he found the keeper's cottage. The keeper was in the garden, stringing weasels and crows onto a gibbet by the gate, and as the fisherman approached, he said, 'You be looking for the Old King of Corfe.'

The fisherman looked at him gratefully and said, 'Those words are as welcome as a full net of mackerel; can you tell me where he is?'

'Wait,' said the keeper, 'I must tell you that the Old King of Corfe is the most powerful magician in the country, and he is holding your son with a magic spell; he has turned him into a dove; but I can tell you how to get your son back.'

Then the fisherman trembled, and thanked the keeper with all his heart, and then he fainted and fell to the ground. The keeper took him into the cottage, sat him by the fire, and gave him food and drink until, at last, the old fisherman was able to talk. After a few days he was ready to move on to try to find his son. The keeper pointed down a track that led further into the forest and told the fisherman that at the end of the track was a great thick thorn hedge and that behind the hedge was a ruined castle. He told the fisherman to go into the courtyard and look up, and that there he would see a flock of doves, and that the fisherman's son was one of those fourteen doves. The fisherman almost broke down again, and he said, 'But how am I going to know which dove and how can I get him back? I'm a fisherman, not a magician!'

The keeper told him that one dove would be flying lower and slower than all the rest, and that dove was his son; and if he pointed out the dove to the Old King of Corfe, he would be obliged to let the boy go back to his rightful father.

Then the fisherman thanked the keeper and set off further into the depths of the wood. And sure enough, there was the thick thorn hedge and the ruined castle, and when the fisherman stepped through a hole in the wall into the courtyard, he could see a flock of fourteen doves flying around the battlements; and one was flying lower and slower than all the rest.

Just at that moment, out came the Old King of Corfe and he said, 'I've been expecting you; if you can tell me which of those doves is your son, you can have him back.'

Then the fisherman pointed and said, 'It's that one!' and the dove circled and landed at his feet, and turned back into the boy. And the fisherman took his son by the hand and together they ran out of the castle, back through the thorn hedge and away down the track, and they didn't stop until they were many miles away.

Then the boy said to his father, 'The Old King of Corfe is the most powerful magician in the country, but he has taught me all he knows, all his spells; and in an old book in the castle library I found some spells that even the King doesn't know, so I think I can beat him, but you will have to help me.

Take me to a small market town in the middle of Dorset and when we get there I will change myself into a greyhound with a silver collar, and I want you to walk me around the market place. Everyone will want to buy me, but don't sell me to anyone except the Old King of Corfe, and when you do sell me, don't sell the collar; I will be that collar, and once he has gone I can turn back into myself.'

Well, the old fisherman didn't understand much of this, but he did as the boy asked, and they made their way to Blandford Forum. When they got there the boy turned himself into a beautiful greyhound with a silver collar, and everyone admired the dog and offered the fisherman lots of money to buy it; but he refused every offer until along came the Old King of Corfe wanting to buy the dog. The fisherman said, 'You can buy the dog, but the collar is precious to me; I couldn't sell the collar.'

The King said that was fine, and that he didn't need the collar, as he had plenty of those at home. So the fisherman sold the dog to the King, and when the King had gone, the collar turned back into the boy and he said, 'We've beaten him once, but to break the spell we must beat him twice. This time, I shall turn myself into a racehorse with a red leather bridle hung with golden bells. Take me up to the racecourse and ride me around. Everyone will want to buy me, but don't sell me to anyone except the Old King of Corfe, and when you do sell me, don't sell the bridle; I will be that bridle, and once he has gone I can turn back into myself.'

This time the fisherman thought that he understood, and together they went up to Racedown and the boy turned himself into a handsome piebald racehorse with a red leather bridle hung with golden bells. The crowd were stunned by the sight of the wonderful horse and everyone wanted to buy the stallion, but the fisherman refused every offer until the Old King of Corfe came up and demanded to buy it. And the fisherman said, 'I can sell you the horse but not the bridle.'

The King said, 'That's fine, I don't need the bridle; I have plenty of tack back at home; but will you allow me to ride the horse once around the racecourse to make sure he's not lame? Surely you would not refuse that?'

But the fisherman did refuse, and the King offered him twice the money; and still the fisherman refused. And then the crowd began to call out, 'Let him try the stallion; it's only fair!'

And the King offered five times the money; and the fisherman was tempted, and gave him the horse and the crowd cheered. But as soon as the King was on horseback, he'd won, and he turned the horse's head and galloped away, bridle and all, and the crowd stood silent, knowing that something was wrong; the fisherman was in despair at his folly.

The Old King of Corfe rode that horse mercilessly all over Dorset. He rode it across Hod and Hambledon, right up Bulbarrow, over the fields and vales to Eggardon, broke the horse's hooves on the Chesil pebbles, and stumbled along the Ridgeway until, at last, they came down to the banks of the Frome, and the King tied the exhausted horse's bridle to a bush by the river and fell fast asleep under a tree.

As soon as the King was asleep the horse began to stir and tug at the bridle; and at last the leather stretched just enough for the horse to pull his head out. But all the bells on the bridle began to ring, and the King woke up just in time to see the horse turn into a sea trout and dive into the Frome to escape. Then the King blew on his horn and his two sons appeared, and all three turned themselves into otters and dived into the Frome to chase the sea trout. They swam downstream and were just about to bite the fish's tail when the fish leapt from the water and turned into a swallow, and flew high up into the sky. Then the otters turned themselves into hawks and flew after the swallow, gaining on him all the time; they were just about to sink their talons into the swallow's back when the bird looked down and saw a lady walking in a garden. The swallow swooped down and turned into a ring on the lady's finger. Then the ring spoke to the Lady and said, 'In a minute three men will come into your garden and dig a pond. As soon as the pond is dug it will fill with water, and there will be rushes and lilies and coloured fish swimming, and they will asK you for me, this ring on your finger, as payment; but don't give me to them. Instead, you must take the ring from your finger and fling it into that bonfire.'

Sure enough, three men came into the lady's garden and dug a pond that was immediately filled with water, rushes, lilies and coloured fish. They asked the lady for her ring as payment, and the lady took the ring from her finger and flung it into the middle of the bonfire.

Then the pond diggers turned themselves into black-smiths with great hammers, and they began to beat the flames in the bonfire to try to break the ring. Then the ring sprang out from the bonfire and turned itself into thousands of grains of corn, scattered all over the garden. The blacksmiths turned themselves into three chickens, and began to eat the corn, grain by grain, until there was only one grain left, and all three chickens closed in on the grain, eyes glinting in triumph. And then the grain turned into a fox and bit their heads off.

Then the fox turned back into the boy, and he left the garden and made his way back to Swanage, got into the boat and sailed out to sea. And as far as I know, he's fishing there still.

The Isle of Purbeck has several curious customs still remembered by older inhabitants. Stone quarries can still be found between Corfe and Swanage, but previously there were many more, governed by ancient laws of possession. This involved the members of the Royal Company of Marblers and Stone Cutters kicking a football, formerly a pig's bladder, through the streets of Corfe on Shrove Tuesday all the way to the manor house at Arne, where 1lb of peppercorns was exchanged in return for annual quarrying rights. Early in the twentieth century, people were still being buried in Lulworth with a penny in one hand and a hammer in the other; the penny to pay the entrance fee into Heaven and the hammer to raise the coffin lid. When someone lay dying, the windows and doors of the cottage were left open to ensure an easier passage into the next world; and the pillow of the one about to depart was stuffed with pigeon feathers.

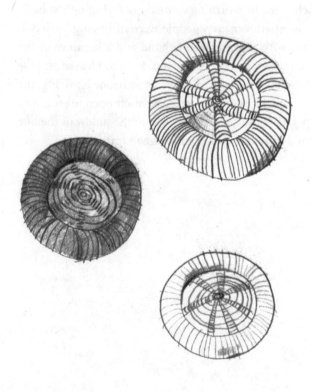

14

Buttons on a Card

Through the cottage windows you can see the tallows burning,
Needles move swiftly round the tiny rings;
Women, men and children busy button making,
In the darkness you can hear a lady sing:
And overnight the makers found their livelihood was lost;

Buttons on a card, very good to sell
Gentlemen and ladies like them very well, like them very well

There's High Tops and Birds Eyes for the waistcoats of gentlemen
Strong cloth buttons for the ones who do the work;
Cartwheels, Mites and Honeycombs stitched and carded carefully
To decorate fine ladies in New York

Trudging through the Dorset lanes to sell their wares on Agents' day,
Buttons in their packs, heavy pattens on their feet;
From Margaret Marsh and Twyford to Gillingham and Shaftesbury,
With goods to sell and old friends to meet

Then a new machine from London could outstrip their hardest labour
And overnight the makers found their livelihood was lost,
Some were forced to emigrate, others joined the parish queue,
Distress was what machine buttons cost

The cottages have vanished, the depots are forgotten,
Progress blew the Button makers clean across the seas
Only Evergreen and Lilac growing in the Twyford hedges
Marks the homes of the button families …

Button making was one of several cottage industries that employed men, women and children, and provided a much-needed boost to family incomes all through the eighteenth and into the nineteenth century. It was particularly widespread in the north Dorset villages around Shaftesbury. However, 'doing buttony' was dealt a fatal blow by a Danish button machine first exhibited at the Great Exhibition in 1851, and the collapse of the industry caused considerable distress in the Blackmore Vale at the time. Various attempts were made to revive the trade, and the skill of making the most characteristic type, the Cartwheel, is still alive. High Tops, Birds Eyes, Mites and Honeycombs were all different types of buttons made to order in the county. I wrote this song for my mother, Beryl Laycock, who was skilled at Dorset feather stitchery and button making.

15

AUCTION OF
CONTENTS

'Auction of Contents' – an old village home,
And the poor lady dead who had lived there alone,
And the floor, that she's always kept spotlessly clean
Was muddied by wellington boots tramping in.

The road outside jammed up with Volvos and trucks,
The dealers buzzing, like flies on the muck;
'Poor, sorry stuff,' they said, 'No, not impressed.'
Then, 'Good God! Look Sadie! A Chippendale chest!'

The auctioneer parted the crowd with his belly,
He fed rather often, resembled a jelly.
He nodded to neighbours, scowled at the rest,
And propped himself up on the Chippendale chest.

'A hot water bottle with cover, complete.'
'That'll do for my man; he's got very cold feet!'
They stared and they sniggered, the hammer came down,
'Name, please, my good woman.' She answered, 'Jane Brown.'

'A good kitchen table with Formica top,
A three-legged stool, and a fine squeezy mop.'
'I can stand on the stool while I mop up the floor,
And a nice bit of Fablon will brighten those drawers.'

'Lot 10, an old loofah, and leaky tin bath.'
She paid fifty pence, and announced with a laugh,
'I can scrub his broad back while he sits by the fire!'
The auctioneer gulped, and began to perspire.

'You're extravagant, madam!' he shook his bald head.
'Oh, no, I'm investing quite wisely,' she said.
'I never buy new, when seconds will do;
I find that used things are more cosy, don't you?'

'Lot number 20, a broken TV!'
She paid fifty pence, 'It's just perfect for me,
I'll have knick-knacks on top, and my papers below,
And I won't need to watch all the rubbish they show!'

'Pepper pot, salt cellar, mustard tin too.'
'I'm warm and I'm spicy,' she told him; 'Are you?
Ever since I was young I've loved anything hot!'
The auctioneer sweated, and knocked down the lot.

'Get on with it, do!' yelled a voice from the door.
'We've put up with this drivel an hour or more.
Time's money, you know, and what we want best
Is lot number 80, the Chippendale chest.'

The auctioneer frowned, 'A casserole dish,
And a tool for removing the innards of fish!'
'I can cook a good stew,' she told them with pride.
'Ah, God save the dumpling!' the auctioneer sighed.

'Lot 80, the chest, come now, what am I bid?'
The dealer, unchallenged, said, '£300 quid!'
Then his cronies all left, with a nod and a wink,
To settle it later in the pub over drinks.

'Good riddance,' she said, with a smile rather shy,
'The price for that chest I should say was too high;
It was made in the village by old Mr Snook,
From a photo he found in a furniture book!'

The auction was over, the crowds left at last
A Volvo filled up with a chest hurried past.
The auctioneer, gasping, fell into a chair
When he saw his best customer coming downstairs.

'There's one more lot, madam, left here all forlorn,
It's me, in poor order, and very much worn.'
'I'll have you for nothing!' the good lady cried.
'I'm going, I'm going, I'm gone!' he replied.

16

THE DEVIL'S THREE JUMPS

Well, you know not so long ago Dorset was a great place for farmhouse cider – still is around Netherbury and Powerstock; but at one time every village, and many of the farms, had their own cider presses and every autumn the sweet smell of apples being pressed was carried on the wind from village to village. And back then they used all the old local varieties, the Warriors and the Sims Seedlings, so there was a lot of variation in the taste – and quality – of the cider. This particular autumn, in Loders, they'd made a very fine brew, and this chap became terribly fond of it. Every night he was down at the barn drinking, and his wife got fed up with it. So while he was out boozing one night, she went up to the airing cupboard, got out a big white sheet, and hid behind the old holly tree that stood by the gate.

Well, at about eleven o'clock, up the lane he comes, singing away at the top of his voice, and as he came in through the gate she jumped out in front of him with the sheet over her head and screamed out, 'Whoooooooooooo!'

'Hello,' he said, 'who be you?

'Whooooo,' she said, 'I BE THE DEVIL!'

'Oh, be you,' he said, 'then shake hands; I married thy sister!'

It seems that Old Nick was a regular visitor to west Dorset in times past. One day he was making his way to Forde Abbey, intent on tempting a few of the monks into wicked ways; but it was a beautiful sunny day and even the Devil found his customary miserable, bitter state of mind softened by the beautiful surroundings of the abbey as he came into the garden. He was even moved so far as to bend down to sniff the wonderful aromatic scents in the herb garden. Just as he did so, the abbot came out from the cloister and spotted a stranger in the garden, with a bit of a tail showing out from the bottom of his coat and a pair of highly polished red hooves treading on the camomile lawn. Quick as a flash, the abbot stepped up and gave Old Nick a mighty kick up the backside that sent him flying east, bouncing on three hilltops before he ended up sore and bruised at Birdsmoorgate. He made his way in a fine temper down to Lyme Regis, and some people say he's still there, living in a little bungalow and biding his time; and those three hills are still known as the Devil's Three Jumps.

Mind you, before the folk in the rest of Dorset get too smug, Old Nick's activities have been reported all over the county. Not long ago, in Shaftesbury, he called in to join the company at a gambling den in a barn down on French Mill Lane. Men and women were in there, playing cards and staying away from church on Sundays. Nick was delighted to see them and joined in the game; but when he bent down to pick up a card, they saw a cloven hoof under his coat, and they all ran off back up Gold Hill as fast as they could go! On another occasion, he reputedly took a holiday on the Isle of Wight, and instead of spending his time peacefully on Alum Bay filling up little glass phials with coloured sand like any civilised visitor would do, he made his way to the Needles, and amused himself by throwing rocks at Corfe Castle. Much to his annoyance, however, his aim was poor, and he never struck a direct hit, or

even came close. One rock landed at Studland on the heath behind the beach, where it still remains and is called locally the Agglestone Rock. In the end, Old Nick had to wait until the Civil War, when Oliver Cromwell's men completed the job for him at Corfe Castle, thanks to a nasty bit of treachery straight out of Chapter 10 of the Devil's Dirty Deeds Manual.

Most people are wary of Old Nick, but quite a few have stood up to him and given him a taste of his own medicine. One of them was a blacksmith called Old Amos, who lived out Shroton way:

> Here's a health to the jolly blacksmith the best of all fellows,
> Who works at the anvil while the boy blows the bellows;
> Which makes his bright hammer to ride and to fall
> Here's the old Cole and the young Cole and the old Cole and all!
> Twanky dillo twankydillo,
> Twankydillo dillo dillo dillo,
> And a roaring pair of blowpipes
> Made from the green willow!

No one could have called Old Amos a jolly blacksmith; most of 'em would have called him a miserable old so-and-so, and tight as a duck's arse. They all complained about his prices, and the length of time he took to do even the smallest job. But there was nowhere else to go unless you were prepared to go the four miles into Blandford, and if your cart wheel was broken or your horse had thrown a shoe, what could you do? Amos had them all over a barrel. Mind you, there was a softer side to his nature; outside the forge, incongruous amongst the rusty wheel rims and lengths of broken chain, was a wonderful rose bush that flourished longer and more prolifically than any other bush in the village – no doubt due to the ready supply of horse manure that he swept up off the forge floor every day!

Oh yes, Amos was tight, there was no denying it; and he had a temper on him too, hot as his fire, but that didn't stop the village children from creeping into the forge and playing with his hammer and tongs. Some of the boldest would even sit in his best chair for a dare. Over in the corner it was, with old sacks over the arms to keep off the sparks, but it was the most comfortable chair in the village, given to Amos some years before by the squire, when that worthy gentleman was a bit short of ready money and wanted to ride over to Bryanston to see his lady friend late one night.

Anyway, one day Amos was in his forge, hammering away, when an old man looked in the door and asked for a drink of water. Now, in the usual way of things Amos would have gruffly directed him to the village pump on the green, but there was something in the old man's manner that made the blacksmith look up, and invite him into the forge.

'You sit yourself down there, sir,' he said, pointing to his favourite chair, 'and I'll see what I can do.'

Off he went out the back, and came back a few minutes later with a jug and two glasses. 'Lemonade,' said Amos, 'my missus is known for it.'

The stranger drank the lemonade gratefully.

'Thank you, Amos,' he said, 'that was an act of charity: do you know who I am?' Amos replied truthfully that he didn't know the man from Adam. 'Well, you've got the right book!' says the stranger, 'I'm St Peter, and I can offer you three wishes is return for your kindness. What do you want? Consider wisely, because you won't get a chance like this again.'

Amos looked at St Peter and he said, 'Well, it gets right up my nose when the village kids come in here behind my back, playing with my tools and ruining them. I wish that whoever picks up my hammer won't be able to let go of it or stop working until I say so.'

St Peter looked doubtful. 'That's not quite the sort of wish I had in mind,' he said, 'but as you've asked for it, I have to give it to you. What's your second? And kindly make it something nicer!'

'Well,' says Amos, 'for my second wish, it makes me mad when those bloomin' kids come in here and sit in my best chair – not that I mind you sitting in it, sir – so what I wants is that, whoever sits in my chair apart from me won't be able to get out unless I say so.'

'Steady on,' protested St Peter, 'there must be a rule about not granting a wish like that; but as I'm not sure what it is, I suppose I'll have to let you have it. What's your third wish, and please make it something generous and thoughtful.'

'Well,' says Amos, 'it's my rosebush …'

'Ah, lovely!' says St Peter, 'I was admiring it. You want it to smell even sweeter, or bloom longer?'

'No,' says Amos, 'it really gets my pip when the young lovers in the village come by and pick my best roses for their buttonholes before they go canoodling with their sweethearts. What I want is that whoever sniffs my rosebush will be pulled inside and pricked with the thorns until I say that he or she can be let go!'

'Amos, oh Amos,' sighed St Peter, 'those are without doubt the three wickedest wishes I've ever had the misfortune to grant. No good will come of this I'm sure, but I can only hope that you never have cause to use these unpleasant wishes; good day to you.'

And with that he was off down the road, and, as he went, Amos could detect a little halo shining round his head, and he thought to himself, 'Well, I'll be blowed! Maybe there was something in that nonsense after all.'

Meanwhile, down in Hell, Old Nick was busy toasting a recently arrived pair of bankers on a large spit. They were nearly done, and he needed more customers, so he called in his two sons, Roger and Beelzebub. Roger was the younger of the two, and carried a large book of names, addresses and personal information that he'd obtained illegally from an insurance company.

'Right, Roger, look lively; we need more customers or the furnace will go out; who's next on the list? Make it someone really evil.'

Roger consulted the oracle. 'Well, Dad, there's that old blacksmith at the crossroads – goes by the name of Amos; everyone says he's a mean old devil; he's been on the list for some time!'

'Excellent!' roared the Devil, giving the bankers a final twist. 'Go and get him, Roger!'

Beelzebub was really annoyed. 'No way, Pa!' he whined. 'It should be me. That little oik couldn't bring home a cow pat, let alone a blacksmith!'

'Silence!' screamed the Devil, 'he's got to learn; off you go Roger!'

Roger flushed, but because he was red all over it didn't really show. 'Did you really mean it Daddy?' he cried, 'I can go up and get a soul myself? Hooray!'

'Yes, it's time you went out into the world and made your own way,' said the Devil paternally, 'just don't let me down, or it'll be you on this spit tomorrow.'

So off went Roger. He polished up his horns and hooves, sharpened the point on his tail, and shot up through a drain, landing right in the smith's forge just as Amos was about to douse a red-hot wheel rim in a trough of water.

'Amos! Amos! Prepare yourself,' said Roger, as impressively as he could, 'you've got to come with me down to the fiery furnace!'

Amos just looked up, spat in the water, and said, 'I'm not quite ready, youngster; grab hold of this hammer and help me get this wheel rim on, or there'll be all hell to pay!'

So Roger grabbed the hammer, and the hammer began to work fifteen to the dozen, and the little devil couldn't let go or stop. It was all that Amos could do to keep him supplied with red-hot iron, and that day Roger made more horse shoes, wheel rims and ornamental fenders than the black-smith had made in the last six months. All night he was at it, sweating and cursing, and at last he begged Amos to allow him to stop.

'On one condition,' said the wily old smith. 'That you clear off back down to your daddy, and tell him not to bother me any more.'

So it was that later that day Roger reappeared in Hell empty-handed. Beelzebub sniggered, and the Devil looked as if he was about to explode. 'Well Roger?' he growled. 'Explain yourself!'

So Roger told the whole sorry saga of how the smith had outwitted him with the hammer, and the Devil looked at his eldest son. 'Alright,' he said, 'go to it; and whatever you do, don't touch that hammer!'

Beelzebub dressed himself up in his best coat and hat, sharpened his teeth, lit a large cigar and disappeared in a puff of acrid smoke, straight up to the blacksmith's forge. He thought the stink of sulphur and Havana would unnerve the smith, but Amos was used to the smell of hot iron and burning flesh, so he carried on calmly working as Beelzebub twisted and capered around the forge.

'Amos! Amos! Prepare yourself,' said Beelzebub, baring his teeth and leering, 'you've got to come with me down to the fiery furnace!'

'Delighted,' said Amos. 'Sit yourself in that chair and I'll just smarten myself up to go with you. I don't want to let you down by looking scruffy, such a snappy-looking dresser as you are.'

Beelzebub sat in the chair and took out a small hip flask. The blacksmith came back in his best Sunday suit, but Beelzebub found he couldn't get out of the chair. No matter how much he struggled and swore, it was no good; he was a prisoner. 'Oh dear, what a shame,' said Amos sweetly. 'If you can't get out to show me the way, I can't go!'

And in the end there was nothing for it but for Beelzebub to agree to leave Amos be, and go back to Hell empty-handed. The Devil was incandescent with rage when he heard the news.

'If you want a job doing properly, do it yourself,' he spluttered, and, placing both his sons in a large cauldron of boiling oil, he shot up to Shroton in a poisonous cloud of methane.

Amos was outside the forge tending his rose bush.

'Amos! Amos! Prepare yourself,' said Old Nick, in a voice that made the whole forge tremble and the window crack.

'You've got to come with me down to the fiery furnace!'

Amos continued with his pruning. 'Well, we've got the top man at last,' he said, 'I suppose you mean business. I'll just take these roses in to the wife, and then I'll be with you. Do you grow roses yourself?'

The Devil looked at the bush. 'Well, yes, as a matter of fact I do,' he said. 'Mostly tea roses and the occasional climber. Of course, it's rather hot down below, and I don't have the ready supply of horse manure that you have; and I've been plagued with blackfly this year – rather a poor show.'

'Yes,' agreed Amos, 'well, if you'll just deadhead this bush for me, I'll pop these in to the missus, and be right with you.'

'Right-ho,' says Old Nick, and takes up the secateurs. But as soon as the touched the bush, it dragged him inside and began to prick him until his skin had more holes in than a cullender. Then Amos and his wife came out and emptied salt over him, which only made the wounds smart even more, and made Nick howl like – well, like the Devil. And at last he pleaded with Amos to let him go, and the blacksmith agreed, on condition that Nick renounced any claim to him – which the Devil had to do; and Amos lived on contented for many years.

But, of course, at last he did die, and made his way up to Heaven. He knocked on the pearly gates and St Peter came out. 'Hello,' says Amos nervously, 'remember me?'

'I do indeed,' says St Peter, 'and you can't come in. The boss didn't like those wishes you chose, not one bit. He doesn't think you're suitable. Sorry!' And with that, he shut the gate.

So Amos couldn't go to Heaven or Hell. Instead he found himself a rather nice little place under a spreading chestnut tree somewhere near Sutton Waldron; and as far as I know he's still there.

Finally, it's only right to mention the Dorset Ooser, a curious and grotesque figure that appeared at cottage doors in Melbury Osmund every Christmas. The head, carved from wood, has staring eyes, matted hair, a great clomping mouth full of discoloured teeth, and a huge pair of bull's horns. Carried on a short pole by a man hidden under a long cloak, it must have made a terrifying impression on anyone seeing it through a dimly lit cottage window for the first time. William Barnes knew of the Ooser, and surmised that the name was a corruption of 'the Worse One' – meaning the Devil. Thomas Hardy's mother came from Melbury Osmund, and in his notebooks he recorded the lyrics of a folk song from the village. Maybe it was sung by the party accompanying the Ooser:

Let's go a-shooting says Richard to Robin
Let's go a-shooting says Robin to Dobbin
Let's go a-shooting says John all Alone
Let's go a-shooting says everyone
What shall we shoot?
Let's shoot the Devil
How bring him home?
Borrow a cart
A cart will not do
Borrow a wagon
How get him indoors?
Pull down the door
How shall we boil him?
Put him in the crock
A crock will not do
Borrow a furnace
A furnace will do

So Old Nick ends up back where he came from!

17

GIANT GRUMBLE

Giants have left a vivid impression on the landscape of Dorset. In the days before archaeology revealed that the hill forts were constructed by our Neolithic ancestors, it was widely believed in the county that only a race of giants could have made the mighty structures that top the hills from Hambledon and Hod in the north to Eggardon and Maiden Castle in the south. A race of giant people were said to roam the hills, scooping out the chalk in mighty handfuls to make their curious ringed dwellings, where they would converge to hold stone-throwing contests that terrorised the smaller local inhabitants and littered the landscape with great boulders. One such contest at Cheselbourne ended in tragedy when two giants strove to outdo each other in feats of boulder throwing. The great rocks went further and further south, crashing onto the Ridgeway until, at last, with a tremendous effort, the strongest giant flung a mighty boulder right over Weymouth into the sea, and there it is to this day, called the Isle of Portland. The other giant was so disappointed that he collapsed and died on the spot: the crowd that had cheered on the contestants so enthusiastically fell silent. One by one they picked up rocks, gently covered the dead giant, and placed a great capstone on the top; and there it remains in the middle of the field, and is still known as the Giant's Grave.

After that the giants made their way towards the coast. One of them remained on the hillside above Cerne Abbas, where for many years he was a terrible nuisance to the smaller folk who had settled to farm the area. Being a giant, he had a great appetite, and would come down at night to take their sheep and cattle. Eventually he grew so bold that he would stride around taking what he pleased, with a great club in one hand and a long cloak in the other, which he would fling over his prey before carrying it back up to the top of the hill. One day he got so greedy that he ate a whole field of cows, and fell asleep on the hillside above the village, lulled by the smell of the thyme in the sunshine. The villagers took their chance and crept up with ropes to pinion the giant to the hillside. Once he was trapped they cut his head off, and the river Cerne ran red with his blood for days. To commemorate their victory over the giant, the villagers carved his outline on the hillside, and there he remains to this day, a mute reminder of an older and wilder Dorset. And some say that was the last time giants were seen in the county – because when the rest of the Dorset giants saw what had happened to their comrade, they took the hint and all moved west to Cornwall.

A less bloodthirsty story from Portesham concerns a young Dorset giant, Giant Grumble.

Giant Grumble was always hungry. Every morning he would come down to his breakfast and shout, 'I am Giant Grumble; you can hear my tummy rumble!'

'Yes, I can,' said his mother. 'What would you like for breakfast, Giant Grumble?'

The youngster replied, 'I want porridge.'

'Pardon?' said his mother.

'I want porridge.' said Giant Grumble, rather louder this time.

'I beg your pardon?' said his mother.

But Giant Grumble just bellowed, 'I WANT PORRIDGE!'

'Well, if you're going to be as rude as that, you can't have any,' said his mother; and instead she handed him a large yellow key. 'Go upstairs, and open the yellow cupboard.'

Giant Grumble knew better than to disobey his mother, so he trudged up the stairs and opened up the yellow cupboard. Inside was a large pair of yellow boots. They looked about the right size, so he sat down and pulled them on, and then he noticed that on one of the boots was a label that said 'One Mile Boots'. Giant Grumble didn't know what that meant, but he soon found out, because when he stood up and took one step, he went one mile, which was a big step even by giant standards. When he'd taken two steps he was two miles away, and after twenty steps he was right in the middle of Dorset, and then he saw a village shop. Displayed in the windows were all sorts of fruits and vegetables; Giant Grumble looked and licked his lips, and thought to himself, 'Apples, oranges and pears. That's what I'll have for breakfast.'

So he banged on the door and the shopkeeper said, 'Good morning young sir; can I help you?'

Giant Grumble roared out, 'I want apples, oranges and pears.'

To which the shopkeeper said, 'Pardon?'

Again the giant roared, 'I want apples, oranges and pears.'

'I beg your pardon?' said the shopkeeper.

Giant Grumble was furious, 'I WANT APPLES, ORANGES AND PEARS!'

But the shopkeeper was not intimidated by this display of temper. 'Well, if you're going to be as rude as that, I won't serve you!' she said, and shut the door, and hung up a little sign that said 'Closed for Lunch'. Giant Grumble had to go all the way home, put the yellow boots back in the cupboard, and that night he went to bed very hungry.

Next morning Giant Grumble came down for breakfast, and he was starving. 'I am Giant Grumble; you can hear my tummy rumble!'

'Yes, I can,' said his mother. 'What would you like for breakfast, Giant Grumble?'

The youngster replied, 'I want porridge.'

'Pardon?' said his mother.

'I want porridge.' said Giant Grumble.

'I beg your pardon?' said his mother.

Giant Grumble just bellowed, 'I WANT PORRIDGE!'

'Well, if you're going to be as rude as that, you can't have any,' said his mother; and instead she handed him a large red key. 'Go upstairs, and open the red cupboard.'

So there was nothing for it; Giant Grumble went upstairs, grumbling to himself. But like all children, he was curious, so he tried the red key in the lock, and the red cupboard opened, and inside was a fine pair of red boots. He tried them on and they fitted perfectly. He stood up and noticed a label on one of the boots, and this time the label said 'Two Mile Boots'. With one step he went two miles; with ten steps he went twenty miles; and before you could say:

Fee Fi fo Fum
I Smell the Blood of an Englishman;
Be he Alive or be he Dead,
I'll Grind his Bones to make my Bread

… he'd walked right up the country into Scotland. He looked around him, sniffed, and smelt the most delicious smell. 'Ah, fish and chips! That's what I'll have for breakfast.'

So he went up to the shop and shouted in through the door-way: 'I want fish and chips.'

'Pardon?' said the owner.

'I want fish and chips.'

'I beg your pardon?'

'Don't you understand plain English?' said Giant Grumble rudely, 'I WANT FISH AND CHIPS!'

'Well, laddie, if ye're going tae be sae rude as that, ye can't have any,' replied the owner briskly; and he went inside, shut up the shop, and hung up a little notice on the door which said 'Gone to Lunch'. So there was noth-ing for it but for Giant Grumble to go home, still hungry. He put the boots back in the cupboard, and that night he could scarcely sleep at all. His belly rumbled so loud that houses shook all over Dorset, and ships were driven onto the Chesil by the waves at sea.

Next morning he came downstairs in a terrible temper. 'I am Giant Grumble; you can hear my tummy rumble!'

'Yes, I can; it's kept most of Dorset awake all night,' said his mother. 'What would you like for breakfast, Giant Grumble?'

Again the youngster replied, 'I want porridge.'

'Pardon?' said his mother.

'I want porridge,' said Giant Grumble.

'I beg your pardon?' said his mother.

But Giant Grumble just bellowed, 'I WANT PORRIDGE!'

'Well, if you still haven't learnt your lesson, you can't have any,' said his mother; and instead she handed him a large blue key, telling him to go upstairs and open the blue cupboard.

'Yellow cupboards, red cupboards and now blue cup-boards; I don't want cupboards, I WANT PORRIDGE!'

'Do as you're told,' said his mother quietly; and there was something in her tone of voice that got through to the angry

giant, so he turned, went upstairs, and opened the blue cupboard. Inside was a pair of blue boots. He put them on, and
they fitted perfectly. One of them had a label that read 'Five
Mile Boots'. Now, the thing with Five Mile Boots is that, not
only can you walk five miles with every step, you can also
walk on water. Giant Grumble walked down to Weymouth
in two steps. He walked across to France, down to Italy, and
then through Greece and Turkey until, at last, he came to a
hot country called Lebanon. He stared at the date palms, and
then sniffed. He smelt the most delicious smell coming from
a nearby house. He looked in through the window and saw
a woman doing two jobs at the same time. With one hand
she was making scones, placing them on a baking tray, and
putting them into an oven; with the other hand she was stir-
ring a large bowl of thick clotted cream. Giant Grumble's eyes
widened, and he licked his lips, 'I want some of those,' he said.

The lady said, 'Pardon?'

Giant Grumble said, 'I want some of those.'

The lady said, 'I beg your pardon?'

Giant Grumble bellowed, 'Are you stupid? Don't you
understand me? I WANT SOME OF THOSE!'

'Well, if you're going to be as rude as that, Giant Grumble,
I certainly won't give you any,' she replied, and closed the
shutters. Giant Grumble went away in a huff, and sat under
the largest palm tree. He thought hard about everything that
had happened over the last three days; and at last he had an
idea. He went over to the house and tapped politely in the
shutters. The lady opened the window and looked at him.
'Yes?' she said.

'I want some of those please,' said Giant Grumble hopefully.

A smile broke over the lady's face. 'Why, of course you
can, Giant Grumble!' she said. Sit down over there and I'll
bring them out when they are ready.'

First of all she brought out a large, brightly coloured tablecloth and tied it round his neck for a bib. Then she brought out a silver try, piled high with fresh scones, clotted cream, jam, honey and a pot of tea. Giant Grumble couldn't decide whether to put the cream on the scones first, or the jam; so in the end he tried them both ways, and each way was equally delicious. He didn't stop eating until the food was all gone, and then he thanked the lady and asked her for the recipe for the scones and the cream. Then he set off back home, put the blue boots away in the blue cupboard, and that night, for the first time in three days, he went to bed with a full belly.

Of course, being a giant, the next morning he was hungry again, so he went downstairs. 'I am Giant Grumble; you can hear my tummy rumble!'

'Yes, I can,' said his mother. 'What would you like for breakfast, Giant Grumble?'

The youngster replied, 'I want porridge please.'

'Of course you can, Giant Grumble,' said his mother. She served him up a great steaming bowl of porridge; and when Giant Grumble had finished, he gave his mother the recipe for the scones and clotted cream, and you can probably guess what they had for tea later on that afternoon.

There's bread and cheese up on the shelf

If you want any more, you must sing it yourself

The origin of the story of Giant Grumble comes from Dorothy Coombes of Portesham. The West Country of England and Lebanon are both places where clotted cream is made and enjoyed. Another explanation for the culinary links between the two countries may well be the ancient Phoenician trade between the Levant and Cornwall.

There is a postscript to the Giant's Grave story. In the nineteenth century, a local farmer determined to improve the productivity of his fields, and decided to demolish the Giant's Grave. It was very inconvenient trying to get his new sail reaper around the stones, so he ordered his men to break it up. They were very reluctant to do this, as they were superstitious and held the stone in awe; but the farmer's word was law, so they began to break away the edges of the capstone. By evening, however, they had made little impression on the great stone, so the farmer ordered them to fetch wood and set fire to it, in an attempt to crack the stone with heat. It was so late when the bonfire had finished that the weary workers lay down in the field and went to sleep around the stone.

As the sun rose, the cock crowed, and the men were terrified to see the stone slowly rise, turn round, and settle down again. They ran to the farmer and told him what they'd seen. He scoffed at the story, but no amount of threats or entreaties would persuade any of them to return to the field. So that night the farmer decided to find out the truth of it, and settled himself down to watch. Sure enough, as the cock crowed at dawn the stone rose, turned round, and gently settled itself. The farmer decided there and then it was best to leave it be, and there it remains to this very day.

Despite their early troubles with their giant, the villagers of Cerne Abbas are now rather fond of him. His outline on the hillside is kept clean, and served in the past as a timely warning to other would-be invaders that Dorset folk are not an easy pushover. He is also widely believed to be an aid to fertility, and plenty of couples wanting a child have spent a night up on the giant to ensure a healthy birth. In Victorian times his obvious manhood was something of an embarrassment to visitors of a delicate disposition, and a mother was heard to tell her child that the giant was a tailor with a large pair of scissors in his lap. David Strawbridge, whose father was headmaster of the village school in Cerne during the 1930s, recalled a rhyme that went:

> The giant he looks over us
> A-doing of our work,
> He must be very chilly
> 'Cos he hasn't got a shirt!

18

THE SKIPPER'S TEETH

The Old Skipper had been at sea, man and boy, for more than forty years, and what he didn't know about the waters around Weymouth and Portland wasn't worth knowing. He knew the Race, and the treacherous seas around the

Chesil Beach, and had clung on to the fishing long after most of his contemporaries had given it up as a bad job – and most of the youngsters wouldn't think of taking up such a dangerous and poorly rewarded occupation.

But the Old Skipper stuck at it, even though his hearing was going, he'd lost most of his teeth, and eventually even his eyesight wasn't what it used to be. But he could still get by; he knew that if he was off Portland Bill in the *Eliza Sue*, and he held up three fingers, and the red and white lighthouse on the Bill was on the right, and Pulpit Rock was on the left, then he was in exactly the right place to catch conger over a wreck.

Well, lately he'd been taking out parties of sea anglers to fish the wreck, and the week before he'd done so well that he'd bought himself a splendid new set of false teeth. They made him feel like a new man. On this particular morning, he was taking out a party of fishermen from Weymouth Police Station. They left early to catch the tide, and on the way out the Skipper fried up breakfast. The Skipper was famed for his fry-ups, but on this occasion something went badly wrong; the bacon and eggs tasted disgusting, and all the policemen surreptitiously slipped their breakfast over the side into the briny. Even the Old Skipper couldn't stand the taste of his own bacon and eggs, and so he took out his wonderful new false teeth to wash the taste away in the sea. Just at that moment, one of the policemen tapped him on the shoulder and said, 'Are we there yet, Skipper?'

Well, the Skipper, without thinking, held up three fingers to check, and dropped his false teeth over the side; and down they went to the bottom of the sea.

Now one of these policemen was a bit of a prankster and thought he would play a little joke on the Skipper, and so he turned and removed his own false teeth, and tied them onto the end of his fishing line. Dropping the 'catch' into the sea and unwinding his line, he suddenly said, 'Skipper! Skipper! I've got a bite!' Reeling in, he proudly declared, 'Look Skipper, I've caught your teeth for you!'

Well the Old Skipper he just untied the line, put the teeth in his mouth, moved his jaws around, and then said, 'Nope, they're not mine,' and flung the teeth back into the sea!

As a postscript to this tale, which was told to me in Winterborne Whitechurch, a couple were on holiday in Weymouth and went for a swim in the bay. The man walked out a long way and began swimming, but lost his false teeth in the sea and couldn't find them. The following day he went swimming in exactly the same spot, and saw something glinting on the seabed … and there were his teeth!

The Chesil Beach or Bank is one of the most dramatic natural features in the country, and one of the real glories of Dorset. Many people consider the view from the top of the hill looking east over Abbotsbury, with St Catherine's Chapel below and the great sweep of Chesil curving round to Portland, to be the finest sight in Dorset – and that's saying something. To be on Chesil in the teeth of a winter storm is to experience the awesome power and ferocity of the sea, and many shipwrecks in the bay testify to the danger of the coast; a danger which continues to this day. Just inland, at Portesham, the villagers were well accustomed to telling the sea conditions and incoming weather from the sounds of the drawing pebbles in the evening. In May time the fishing boats at Abbotsbury are still garlanded; the garlands of flowers are carried in procession around the village and then are taken out in the boats and flung into the sea to ensure a good

catch in the forthcoming season. Nowadays, not many fishermen believe that Luck or Lucky Stones (stones with a hole
right through them) tied in the front of a fishing boat will
prevent drowning; but one old sailor in Bradford Peverell,
an ex-Royal Navy man, recently produced just such a stone
from his pocket, and said that it had seen him unscathed
through Dunkirk in the Second World War and he would
never be parted from it.

All through the summer, fishermen at sea and anglers on
Chesil bring mackerel ashore; and there are still locals who
remember the catches made off the beach with seine nets,
when shoals of sprats were sighted. The long rectangular net
was shot from the beach and towed by a rowing boat around
the shoal, and the other end was brought ashore. Then it was
all hands on deck to haul in the seine, and frequently the
beach was covered with a shining mass of sprats.

Word quickly got round when these red-letter days
occurred. On one particular occasion, a young farmer's son
from Portesham was on the beach at Abbotsbury, helping
to haul in the seine net. All the larger fish were scooped up,
iced and packed, but many of the smaller ones were just
left behind. He asked the fishermen if he could take some
home for tea, but he had nothing to carry them in. Being
a resourceful chap and not thinking, he took off his jacket,
tied the sleeves together, filled it up with sprats, fastened
the buttons and carried his haul proudly home to mum.
However, the delight she felt in seeing the free supper was
rather cancelled out by the prospect of having to try remove
the overwhelming smell of fish from the boy's jacket.

19

A Trafalgar Tale

It was a cold November night and the fog had come down early. Around the narrow streets of Weymouth it whirled and eddied, creeping into every doorway, causing those folk that were still out to button up their coats and hurry along the lanes with their heads down. The White Hart was crowded. The regular crew of townsfolk and fishermen in the public house was boosted by a few late holidaymakers, and passengers from a Channel Islands packet that had just docked. Over in the corner of the pub two old sailors sat yarning, spinning out two small tankards of beer. Bill was bearded, an ex-naval man, still wearing the tattered remains of the jacket he'd worn when discharged from his last ship twenty years before. Charlie Symes was the older of the two, a fisherman, ferryman and one-time smuggler.

'Good evening, gentlemen, mind if I join you?' They looked up. The stranger was a countryman, quite well-to-do by his dress, maybe a farmer or a miller. He was of middle age, becoming stout, but with a healthy look about him, as if he spent most of his time outdoors.

'Aye, sit yourself down,' says Bill, 'we were just thinking of having another drink.'

Taking the hint, the landsman ordered the beer and sat down with them. After some preliminary conversation about the weather and the prospects for the fishing, he admitted a fascination with the sea, and some of the strange tales that were told, particularly by deep-water sailors.

'I was wondering,' he said, 'whether either of you gentlemen ever sailed beyond these waters.'

'That we did,' said Charlie, 'I was in the Newfoundland trade for several years. Shipped from Poole Harbour for Lesters to Trinity, and worked the Grand Banks, and George's Shoals. That was the place for cod! We'd be out in dories as they called 'em, little boats no bigger than the row boats you see in the harbour here, long-lining for cod, and you'd catch 'em as quick as you could pull 'em in. Lor, it would be a fine thing to have some fishing like that round here; only thing like it is when the mackerel come in to the Chesil in the summer, and you can haul 'em out by the bucketful. But, see, because they was so plentiful, there was always plenty of other fishermen after them. The seas round the fishing grounds were that crowded, what with English vessels, and Scottish, and the Irish, and that's not to mention Dutch and Spanish and Yankees and I don't know who else. It was a wonder vessels were not run down more often than they were. And if you think this fog here tonight is bad, you should spend a night in a Newfoundland fog – you can't see your eyeballs in front of your eyes. Lasts for days sometimes, and it's that cold, the ice freezes on all the ropes and sails, even on your beard …

'Aye, every season there were vessels run down, and poor sailors lost, so I don't doubt this story's true, for it was told to me by one of the crew on the vessel in question, and he was a religious man never known to swear or tell a lie; they all called him the Preacher, and he swore to me that this was gospel-true …

'They'd sailed out of St John's one afternoon to fish on George's Shoals, which was always good fishing, but prone to fog. Sure enough, the fog came down just as they was about to launch the dories, so the skipper told 'em to keep the dories swung in, for he couldn't see an inch beyond the schooner's bowsprit. They had port and starboard lamps burning, of course, and set off a signal gun every five minutes. She was scarcely moving at all, running on quarter sail, when suddenly they struck something, and heard shouts and screams; but by the time they'd run to the side and looked over, there was nothing to be seen. The skipper hove to for a while and they all looked around; they had ropes over the side, but not a pull, nothing – not a sound, not a shape in the water. In the end they set sail and moved slowly on until they came to the fishing ground. They were all dismayed by the incident, especially the next day when the fog lifted and they saw a great scrape across the bows of the schooner, and some scraps of rope that were not theirs hanging from the chains.

A few nights later they were out again on George's Shoal, this time under a clear, starry sky. The seas were unusually calm for that part of the ocean and the schooner was hardly moving. They'd had a good day with the dories, and most of the crew were in the snug, drinking and yarning. There was just the Preacher on watch; the skipper had gone below to his hammock. He was suddenly aware of the temperature dropping right away, and he noticed a strange boiling in the seas alongside the schooner. Then all of a sudden, a hand appeared on the rail, and then another; and a fisherman, all dripping wet, hauled himself over the rail without a word, walked past the wheel to the bow of the vessel, and proceeded to keep watch. Then another appeared, and another, all in the same state, dripping wet, white-faced, eyes blank and open wide. Twelve of them there were, and not one of them spoke a word. They just set to and trimmed the sails, and pretty soon the schooner was flying across the water as if she was in a race. One of these sailors seemed to be the skipper. He stood alongside the wheel as close as I am to you, sir.

At this the sailor reached over and touched the landsman on the sleeve, staring intently into his eyes.

'Aye, that was how the Preacher reckoned it. And this fella kept looking down at the compass, and squinting at the sails. He was that close the Preacher could have touched him – but he didn't dare, on account of the weird luminescent hue of his gansey, and the look in his eye, which seemed to be empty of anything at all.

'Well, the Preacher didn't dare to leave the wheel, though it seemed as if he wasn't quite in control of it; for every now and then, the fella alongside would touch it, and it spun in his hands. But they sailed on until the first light of dawn, and the Preacher saw the flash of Trinity lighthouse on the horizon. It was then, without a word, that the sailors left their posts, made their way to the side of the schooner, and disappeared over the side, just as the mate came up from below to change the watch. He was just in time to see the last of them going over the side, and the Preacher said he was eternally grateful for that, for otherwise he would never have been believed by the rest of the crew. That was the Preacher's tale, and he swore until his dying day that it was true. And the other members of the crew agreed, and reckoned that those ghostly sailors were the crew of the vessel they'd run under, come back to show them they meant no harm, and knew it was no fault of theirs.'

The landsman thanked him for his story and, without being asked, fetched another round of drinks. 'A thought-provoking tale,' he said, 'and I don't doubt the truth of what you've told us. How about you, sir?' he turned to the younger sailor. 'Can you top that?'

'No one can top Charlie's yarns,' replied Bill. 'And I was in the senior service, where of course such tale-spinning ain't allowed. But you do hear and see some strange things at sea, there's no denying it, and I've seen my share, I suppose. About thirty years ago I shipped in HMS *Hero* – ship o' the line, 74-gun third-rate. We were appointed to the Southern Station and spent the summer cruising off the West Indies. One particular day we were at anchor off Port Aux Prince, middle of the afternoon, and the sea was as flat as a mill pond. I was on deck along with several others, under an awning, repairing sails. We heard a splash and then a cry from forward and, thinking it was man overboard, we all ran to the side to look and see if we could offer assistance. There, clinging to the port anchor chain, was the strangest figure I ever saw. You might have said he was a man, if he wasn't a fish; and you might have said he was a fish, if he wasn't a man – if you get my drift. He was covered in shells and barnacles, and the hair on his head was so entangled with green and red seaweed, it was impossible to say whether it was really brown or black. He was spouting out water like a whale, and at the same time singing out like a matelot heaving the lead. Well, none of us knew what to do. The marines were up for getting their muskets and taking a shot at him, but the mate was having none of that.

"Stand aside," says he, "let's see if this be a Christian soul or no!" and making his way to the bows he leans over bold as brass and hails the creature with a great, "Ahoy there mate!" Well, to our amazement, there came the distinct response, "Ahoy yerself, matey!"

"What do ye want?" cried the mate.

"Just a word with your Old Man, if I might be so bold," said the merman.

'For by this time we had all decided that he could be no one else. And when we heard him say that, we knew for sure he was some kind of Son of the Sea; for who else would know to call the captain the Old Man?'

'Well, the captain was duly sent for and took the trouble to arrive in full dress rig. He greeted the visitor courteously, and enquired whether he could be of assistance.

"That ye can, Captain," said the merman. 'You've dropped yer anchor right in front of my berth down below. The fluke of yer anchor has stove in my front door, and my wife is trapped inside, along with me four nippers."

'The captain lost no time in ordering the anchor to be slowly raised. We all manned the capstan with a will, and by George we had a job to get that anchor up. When she broke the surface at last the marines gave three hearty cheers, and applying the brake to the capstan, we all ran to the side of the *Hero* to see the sight. There, pinioned on the fluke of the anchor, was the strangest house you ever saw. The walls were made of seashells, and it was thatched in grand fashion with seaweed and wrack. The windows were portholes from wrecked ships, and what was left of the door was a hatch cover from a fourth-rater. On the top was a fine chimney fashioned from a cannon, and if you'll believe me ...'

'THERE WAS SMOKE COMING OUT!' says the landsman, laughing heartily and slapping Bill on the back.

'Damn me, you knew it!' said the sailor ruefully, tossing back his liquor.

'Yes,' says the landsman, 'I heard it years ago; but never told as well as that; thank you!'

'Well, sir,' said Bill, 'since we've entertained you, perhaps 'tis time for you to repay the compliment, and engage us with a yarn of your own.'

'Perhaps I will,' said the landsman thoughtfully, 'but my throat's a bit dry. I'll just get these refilled.' When he returned he looked at his two companions and smiled. 'You won't believe this,' he said. 'Sitting here, I can hardly believe it myself. It seems so long ago, such a long time that it seems like another life. But I don't mind telling you, since you both understand the ways of the sea.

'First of all I should say that I am no sailor. That's not to say I didn't dream of going to sea when I was a boy – who doesn't? And I had an uncle – Uncle Francis – who was a famous sailor.

'He was the only surviving officer when the *Quebec* was set on fire by the French warship *Surveillante* south-west of Ushant. He was picked up from the sea by the enemy wearing only a signet ring and a pigtail ribbon. Of course he soon escaped ... his son Francis got himself tattooed from head to foot and married an Indian queen. Uncle Francis was always a hero for me. He took Captain Hardy on-board his vessel the *Helena* as midshipman.'

The two sailors looked up. Captain Hardy was a great hero to them all – Nelson's captain at Trafalgar, and a local man from Portesham. They'd often seen him walking on the esplanade, and raised a cheer to the great seaman.

The landsman took a drink and continued, 'I went to sea when I was sixteen, on a passage to the West Indies. I was sick the whole way. I can't pretend I enjoyed the first month at all; but gradually I began to get my sea legs, and then when we were in the West Indies, who should be riding at anchor nearby but Captain Hardy himself; he came on-board, and asked to see me. There we were, him in all his splendour and me just a slip of a lad, and he was talking to me about my father's flax mill, and Burton Bradstock, and Rear Admiral Ingram who was in charge of the Sea Fencibles, and my Uncle Francis, and all the other sailors looking on with their mouths open like a shoal of fish!'

'So you're saying that Captain Hardy was a family friend, so to speak?' asked the old sailor.

'Yes, sir, but none of the credit is mine,' said the landsman. 'It was all to do with my father and my uncle Francis. Well, Captain Hardy asked me if I liked life at sea; so what could I say? And when I said that I did, he said he would arrange a place for me on-board HMS *Victory*, and that I should ask my father to write and arrange it when I got back home to Dorset. So that's what I did.'

'You were on the *Victory*?' said the younger sailor incredulously.

'Yes,' said the landsman, 'as midshipman. I went on-board at Portsmouth in September 1805.'

'Six weeks before Trafalgar?'

'Yes,' said the landsman, and stared into his mug. The two sailors looked at him intently, waiting for him to continue. He had them fast now, like a fish on a line. At last he seemed to decide something, and continued.

'Yes, I was midshipman on the *Victory*, along with several others. You'll know of course that a 100-gun ship of the line had several middies. But I was no sailor, not like the real hardened veterans on-board. I was still a little clerk, assistant to the purser, writing lists of supplies and provisions in a ledger. So it went until the middle of October, when we joined the British fleet off Cape Trafalgar, and cruised up and down for days. Nothing happened.'

'That's life in the navy, all right,' agreed Bill, 'weeks and weeks of nothing in particular; I remember it well.'

'Then, at last, one day Captain Hardy calls for me again, and tells me that we are about to go into a great battle, and that I'll have a tale to tell for evermore if I live to see the end of the next day. And that I'm to go down to the cockpit and report to Mr Beattie the surgeon and that my duties in the battle will be to assist him.'

By this time a small crowd had gathered round the table, listening carefully to the landsman's story. It was as if the strength of the testimony had reached out through the fog and fumes to nudge the nearest topers, causing them to hush their laughter and songs, and listen to the Trafalgar tale.

'Twenty-first of October 1805 – that's a date I will never forget. I spent the whole of the battle below decks in the cockpit, so I saw nothing of the fighting, the fire and the fury up on deck. All I saw was the consequences of the action. Man after man brought down moaning and bleeding, to be laid on tables or propped against the bulkheads, waiting to be seen by the surgeon. My job was to give water and lemon to the patient, give them rum, and a piece of wood to bite on. I had to help to hold them down while the surgeon wielded the knife. I saw things that day I never want to see again. By the end of the fight my apron was completely soaked in blood, and the deck was awash with it. I had to get a bucket and sluice it off, lest we slipped over.'

'Begging your pardon, sir,' said Charlie, 'if you was in the cockpit all through the battle, then perhaps you saw Lord Nelson?'

'I did,' said the landsman. 'I was there when he was brought down, covered in a coat. I was there when he was laid against the bulkhead, and Mr Beattie examined him; and I could tell by the look on his face that 'twas all up for the admiral. I was there when Captain Hardy came down to report that the battle was won, and that we had captured eighteen of the French, and our men were on-board; and I was there when the end came, and the chaplain said a prayer over him, and they laid him out and covered him up. I was there, and I saw all that.'

The whole room in the White Hart was silent. Every man and woman watched the landsman as he sat looking into the fire, lost in the memory of what he'd seen.

'And is it true that our admiral was brought home in a leaguer?' asked the old sailor at last.

'True it is,' said the landsman. 'Sewn up in a hammock and preserved in spirits. It was the only way. We were a long time coming back, owing to the great storm, and the contrary winds. We lost most of the prizes we had taken. *Victory* was little more than a wreck. How we got back I'll never know, except that Captain Hardy and the tars of the *Victory* were the best crew that ever sailed.'

'Amen to that,' said the naval man. 'Now sir, we'll drink yer health, for I don't doubt from the modest way you've told your story that it's the truth we've heard from you tonight. But let me ask you one thing, since you was there, and you saw what the rest of us have only wondered about: is it true that the sailors tapped the leaguer, and drank the admiral's health?'

'All I can say is, I never did so myself,' said the landsman. 'But of course, I heard the rumours. If it was done, it was because they loved him, and they hoped by so doing to imbibe just a little of his spirit. That's all I can say!'

Softly a voice began to sing; and soon the whole room had joined in, raising up the old shanty whose words seemed so appropriate:

A drop of Nelson's blood wouldn't do us any harm
And a drop of Nelson's blood wouldn't do us any harm
A drop of Nelson's blood wouldn't do us any harm
And we'll all hang on behind

And we'll roll the old chariot along
We'll roll the old chariot along
We'll roll the old chariot along
And we'll all hang on behind

Richard Roberts, the landsman in this tale, was born in Burton Bradstock. His family and the Hardys of Portesham were close friends. Richard served aboard HMS *Victory* at Trafalgar and recorded his impressions of the action in a diary, which he called his Remarks Book. The book and letters from his family survive still.

In Thomas Hardy's *The Dynasts*, the story of broaching the admiral is retold by citizens and sailors in a Budmouth inn. Another tale, made into a poem by Charles Causley, relates how the dead admiral rose up in the leaguer, pushing off the lid and giving the sentry the scare of his life.

20

THE POOR WORKHOUSE BOY

The cloth was laid in the workhouse hall,
The greatcoats hung round the whitewashed walls;
And all the paupers were blithe and gay
A-keeping their Christmas holiday;
And the Master he cried with a roughish leer
'You'll all get fat on your Christmas Cheer!'
But one by his looks he seemed to say
'I must have more soup on this Christmas Day.'
Oh, the poor workhouse boy,
Oh, the poor workhouse boy!

At length all of us to bed was sent
The boy was missing! In search we went.
We sought him above, we sought him below,
We sought him with faces of grief and woe.
We sought him that hour, we sought him that night,
We sought him in fear, and we sought him in fright;
And a young pauper cried 'I know we shall
Get jolly well whopped for losing our pal!'
Oh, the poor workhouse boy,
Oh, the poor workhouse boy!

We searched in each corner, each crevice we knew,
We looked in the yard, we peeped up the flue
We searched in each kettle, each pan, each pot,
In the water butt looked, but we found him not.
The weeks passed by, we was all of us told
As how someone had said he'd been burked and sold;
When the Master goes out, the parishioners wild cry
'There goes the Cove who burked the poor child!'
Oh, the poor workhouse boy,
Oh, the poor workhouse boy!

At length the soup coppers repairs did need,
A coppersmith came, and there he seed
A dollop of bones a-grizzling there
In the leg of the britches the boy did wear.
We drained the coppers, but nought we found
But an old ragged shirt and a small toothcomb;
And we all of us says, and we says it sincere-
'Twas the best soup we'd tasted for many's a year!
Oh, the poor workhouse boy,
Oh, the poor workhouse boy!

Now all you young people, a warning take
From this here workhouses' boy's mistake;
If he'd never done wrong he'd have always done right,
And I shouldn't need to lament him tonight.
So don't be rambunctious, nor put a stopper
On what yer pa and yer ma think is proper;
Nor at robbing of kettles and pans don't stoop,
'Cos fat boys and bones makes the best 'tater soup!
Oh, the poor workhouse boy,
Oh, the poor workhouse boy!

This recitation was performed by Sam Cowell (1820–1864), one of the pioneer performers of the music hall. He specialised in comic parodies of folksongs and popular poems. This story is based on *The Mistletoe Bough*, a popular carol in Victorian times which also exists as a tale told about several houses in England. The story goes that a bride, playing hide-and-seek on her wedding day, was imprisoned in an old oak chest and not found for several years. The image of a skeleton in a bridal gown had a powerful appeal for the Victorians. The Dorset connection is that Sam Cowell, who had just endured a strenuous tour of the eastern United States during the worst winter of the American Civil War, was in terminal decline due to a combination of alcoholism and consumption. He gave his last performance in the Crown Hotel in Blandford Forum and died in East Street shortly afterwards. He is buried in the town cemetery.

21

THE ABBEY BELLS

John Dunkley was a waggoner, known to everyone as 'Slowly'. That was because he owned the biggest, heaviest and slowest wagon in Shaston, and was the most common cause of blockages and hold-ups in the narrow lanes around the ancient hilltop town. Every morning from his yard in Enmore Green he would harness up a pair of oxen to the great wooden cart and off they would go, all over the Vale of Blackmore, to fetch and carry for the local farmers, millers and gentry. Despite the size of his wagon and the oxen that pulled it, Slowly ran the whole operation himself, except for a stable boy whose job it was to tend to the beasts at the beginning and end of the day, and then to accompany the wagon on its travels. Slowly had at one time employed more boys, but he found that they spent too much time playing and not enough working; as he put it, 'One boy's a boy, two boys are half a boy, and three boys are no boy at all!'

Skippet was Slowly's current boy, and even the old man had to admit he knew his job. He took a great delight in feeding and rubbing down the oxen until their thick coats shone, and polishing up the bells that hung on their harnesses. The boy would leap out of the wagon whenever the gradient got steep – which is most of the time around Shaston – and was always on hand to chock the wheels with wedges if there was any danger of the wagon slipping on Tout Hill, or especially coming round the corner on St John's Hill.

So that was how Slowly's days were passed, carrying heavy goods that no one else could manage to and from the abbey town. His work was timed to the abbey bells that rang out across the vale throughout the day, calling the faithful to prayer, and allowing the townsfolk to regulate their businesses and lives. Slowly himself was not a particularly religious man, though he placidly accepted the daily and seasonal offices of the Church. Out in the vale, however, passing a sacred spring or a venerated oak, he would carefully make his offerings to the other Gods. 'No point in offending anyone, that's my motto,' he would say, as he dropped a small coin into the water. Often on a summer's evening, returning on the wagon with a light load, the harnesses jingling and the abbey bells ringing out, Slowly would hum a little tune to himself, and reflect that there were worse places to live. But on a winter's night, with the whole town shrouded in icy fog, and the wheels slipping in the muddy ruts of the lanes, he would curse the weather, the roads and the constant demands of the farmers and millers that sent a poor man out in December frost.

Slowly's most regular employment came from the abbey. The same applied to most of the merchants in the town. But no one else could manage the heavy goods that he could, so the abbey steward was a regular visitor to the yard in Enmore Green.

Slowly scarcely looked up when Jack Brickell came in this particular morning. Cheerful sort Jack was; he usually looked as though he had his own key to the abbey wine cellars, which of course he did. But on this occasion he was worried, and looked around him to make sure they were alone before he spoke.

'Got a job for you, Slowly,' he says, 'but you must keep it quiet, and it must be done by night.'

Slowly sucked his teeth, 'That'll be extra,' he said.

The steward kept his temper. 'Naturally,' he said, 'and I'm sure the goods will be adequately secured this time!'

Slowly accepted the blow; the steward was referring to an unfortunate incident on Gold Hill the previous summer, when a rope fixing had broken, and several barrels of Flemish wine had rolled off the wagon and smashed on the cobbles.

'What's the load?' asked Slowly, changing the subject.

'I'm paying you extra, Master Dunkley, to undertake this task with the utmost discretion. It's the two great bells – Intercede and Ave Maria – we're having them swung down from the tower tomorrow. You are to take them on your wagon, and carry them by the least visible route to East Compton.'

Slowly was puzzled. The tiny church at East Compton already had a bell, and the tower was certainly not strong enough to take the two great abbey bells.

'I'm speaking to you in the strictest confidence,' said the steward. 'My Lady Abbess has particularly asked that you undertake this task. She is daily expecting Master Cromwell's commissioners to come to take an inventory of all the abbey's possessions, and she fears that the bells will be broken up and sold for scrap. The thought of such sacrilege prompts her to call on a good-hearted fellow like yourself to prevent such a desecration from taking place.'

Slowly rubbed his neck. It was true that other abbeys and monasteries had lost most of their wealth; some had even been burned to the ground, and the monks and nuns driven out. 'Well,' he said at last, 'I shall miss those bells ringing out as I come home of an evening. 'Tis one of the sounds of Shaston. But I've no desire to see the bells melted down to make cannon or whatever, so I'll do as you ask. Where am I to take them?'

The steward told him that there was a new pond being dug in the corner of the open field under Spreadeagle, just north of the village. Slowly nodded; he'd seen the workings.

'Take them there,' said Master Brickell. 'There will be men waiting with ropes and beams to unload the bells into the hole. They will be buried straight away, and there they will lie until such time as it is safe to uncover them, and, God willing, restore them to their rightful place.'

'And might I be so bold as to enquire who's to get the job of bringing them back?' asked Slowly hopefully.

The steward laughed, 'Never miss a trick do you, Slowly? If these hard times mend quicker than I expect them to, and you and I are still above ground, I'll be delighted to call on your services again; but I wouldn't hold my breath if I was you. Now, you'll need your strongest oxen …'

'That'll be Speedwell and Cherry,' Slowly interrupted.

'… and you'd better bring that lad of yours along to do the chocks. You'll bring your wagon to the bottom of Gold Hill after curfew, muffle the wheels and tie up the harness bells. The abbey bells will come down Gold Hill on sleds, and then we'll slide them onto your wagon. I'll have twenty men standing by to haul on the ropes. You'll go down French Mill, across Melbury into Compton, then up to the field – understood?'

Later that night, after curfew, Slowly and Skippet made their way through St James to the bottom of Gold Hill as quietly as it was possible for the wagon and two oxen to go. The axles were freshly greased, the chains and harness were bound round with rags, and Slowly and Skippet were wrapped up in cloaks, with their hats pulled down. All went well at first: the bells were carefully slid over the cobbles on beams and set on the back of the wagon, while Slowly anxiously watched the axles and the braces. Then the bells were lashed securely in place and covered with old horse blankets, and the helpers vanished into the winding streets and back up the hill. Slowly and Skippet were alone with their load, and gingerly they edged the oxen across the road and into the lane that headed out of Shaston down into the vale. All that could be heard was the creaking of the cart and the blowing of the oxen as they took the strain.

'Where you going John Dunkley, and what you got in that cart?' Slowly and Skippet looked at each other – they'd completely forgotten about Granny Rideout, the nosiest woman in St James – and that was saying something. Granny's cottage was conveniently placed at the top of the lane into the town, and nothing went by without her noticing it. Slowly decided the only thing to do was to brazen it out.

'Good evening, Granny,' he says politely, raising his hat. 'I don't want to alarm 'ee, but we're on abbey business – that's why we're out after curfew. We got two bodies here, dead ones from the infirmary. Pilgrims they be, from France, got the dropsy plague terrible bad and swelled to twice their normal size. 'Tis terrible infectious; we're only safe because the Lady Abbess has blessed us. I'd go inside if I was you, and burn some rosemary and say yer prayers.'

Granny gave a strangled squawk and disappeared from the window. Slowly heaved a sigh of relief, touched the goad on the oxen shoulders, and on they went down the hill.

All went well for a couple of hours until they got to the river at the bottom, where the lane was all rutted, and the mud came halfway up the wheels. Then suddenly the wagon jolted to a halt. Skippet and Slowly leapt out, thinking she was stuck fast. Then they saw a shadowy shape, big and bulky, right in front of them on the bridge.

'It's Turner's bull,' whispered Skippet. 'He's a fierce one, no ring in his nose neither.'

The bull glared at the oxen, and the oxen stared impassively back. For several minutes nothing could be heard but the angry, rapid breathing of the enraged bull and the slower, methodical breathing of Speedwell and Cherry. Then, just when Slowly was beginning to think they'd be there all night, the bull began to back away. The oxen strained, the wagon jolted forward, and off they went again. They came to the entrance to Long Meadow, and the bull backed in to let them pass; and then, to their amazement, he slowly knelt down and bowed his head to the ground. 'Well, that beats it all,' said Slowly to Skippet. 'I've heard tell they kneel on Christmas Eve for Our Lord's birthday, but I'd never have believed they'd kneel in the middle of June for the abbey bells!'

'Maybe he was just tired,' suggested Skippet, 'I certainly am.'

They were both tired, and it was the coldest part of the night. They wrapped their cloaks around them, and the oxen jogged steadily on up the hill over the brow of Melbury. The oxen knew the road, and it wasn't long before both man and boy were fast asleep, lulled by the motion of the wagon.

Suddenly a voice rang out, 'Whoo!'

Skippet sat up with a start, 'Sam Skippet yer honour, boy to Master Dunkley, at yer service.'

'Whoo!'

'Master Dunkley, wagon master and carrier of Shaston sir, and working for our Lady Abbe ...'

'Hush boy,' says Slowly, 'tis only an old owl. Here, have some cider and bread.'

Well, after that there was no more excitement. They stopped the wagon in the woods below Compton to feed and water the oxen, and pushed on into the village. As the first red streaks of dawn appeared in the east, they reached the diggings, and the waiting men took off the bells and covered them in soil, so you'd never have known they were there. As the last spadeful was stamped down, the sun came up over Melbury and lit on the empty wagon below.

'Time to head off home I reckon,' says Slowly. 'Come on lad.'

Rather than retrace their steps and risk Granny Rideout again, Slowly decided to take the cart through to Melbury and up into Shaston along the high road. The road at Melbury was very narrow, but the wagon was light now and the going firm.

Just as they were negotiating the bends at Melbury they heard galloping horses behind them, and a horn sounding out, 'Hey you, clear the way, clear the way!'

Slowly looked round severely at the riders; all clad in black they were, their horses and leggings stained with mud. They looked angry.

'You'll have to be patient,' he said, 'this road's narrow. My wagon's wide. I can't turn. Unless you want to ride over the banks, you'll have to follow on; and if you don't want to get muddier than you already are, I suggest you keep yer distance.'

'Look here, you villain,' said one of the riders, a hoity-toity sort of chap with a feather in his hat. 'Do you know who we are? We're Master Cromwell's commissioners.'

'I don't care if you're King Henry himself,' said Slowly, 'this road's narrow. My wagon's wide. I can't turn. Unless you want to ride over the banks, you'll have to follow on; and if you don't want to get muddier than you already are, I suggest you keep yer distance!'

So it was that on the day that Thomas Cromwell's commissioners came to Shaston to seize the wealth of the abbey, they were obliged to follow on in the wake of John Dunkley's wagon. They never did get the bells, but neither did Slowly get the chance to return them. They were lost and forgotten, until they were discovered many years later, and hung in the church tower at St Andrews in Fontmell. The old abbey tower where they used to ring out across the vale is long gone, its stones built into half the houses in Shaston.

Two of the bells at St Andrew's Church, Fontmell Magna, are very old and rare. One has been dated to around 1450, and the inscription reads: *Intercede Pia Pro Nobis Virgo Maria,* which means: Intercede sweetly for us, Virgin Mary.

The other, which is also from the fifteenth century, simply says *Ave Maria.* When I was growing up in the village in the 1950s, the story that the bells came from Shaftesbury Abbey was generally accepted.

22

GEORGE PITMAN AND THE DRAGON

Old George Pitman was coming home late one stormy night across Dunbury Hill. He'd been working late, and he was dog tired as he trudged along head down, trying to keep the weather off his face. Then something made him look up, and he saw a light in the bushes. He couldn't think what it was; there was no house in the area and it was far too wet for a gorse fire. He went to look, and when he got closer he saw that the land had slipped, and there was the entrance to a tunnel, with light streaming out. He could just make out the remains of old brickwork in the entrance, and cracked paving stones on the floor. Being a curious sort, George stepped inside and followed the tunnel. It sloped down into the hill, and the further he went, the brighter the light became. The tunnel got wider and higher, until, at last, it broadened out into a huge cave, way down under the hill. The whole cavern glowed with an eerie green light; and in the middle, coiled up fast asleep, was a great dragon. All green and gold it was, with a great long scaly tail, and sharp black claws on the ends of its legs. That was surprising enough; but what really made George blink was a great heap of gold and silver treasure, protected by the coils of the dragon's tail. Well, you don't see a sight like that every day, do you? George thought to himself, 'Just one of those bits of treasure would keep me and my missus comfortable for the rest of our days.' So he thought he'd take a piece. He tiptoed round to the other side of the cave, away from where he imagined the dragon's head to be, and slowly edged forward towards the end of the dragon's tail, where one particularly rich piece of treasure lay invitingly on the top of the pile. But just as he reached over the dragon's tail, the great creature stirred, and her head appeared where George least expected it. She half-opened one red eye and seemed to stare right at him, as much as to say, 'Don't you dare, George Pitman!' George thought better of it, backed away to the edge of the cave, inched his way carefully around until he came to the entrance to the tunnel, and then turned and ran as fast as he could down the hill right through the village until he reached the pub.

He burst in through the front door as white as a sheet, and it was quite some time before anyone could get a sensible

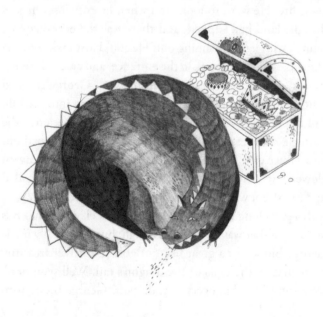

word out of him. But at last, after they'd given him a drop of brandy, sat him by the fire, and made sure it wasn't a death in the family, or a win on the Premium Bond, or the black dog running along by the Winterbourne that several others had seen, they began to get some sense out of him. And George told his story just as I've told it to you.

Well, of course they didn't believe a word of it, but at last Jim Merrifield says, 'Alright George, we'll go and see this tunnel of yours.'

And up the side of Dunbury Hill they went with torches and spades, and a few potato sacks, and the gamekeeper's shotgun – just in case. All around they looked, in the wood, everywhere they could think, but there was no tunnel, no light coming out of the ground, no dragon, no treasure, nothing at all. So it couldn't have been true – could it?

Tales of buried treasure and underground tunnels are widespread in Dorset. Shaftesbury is reputed to have both, with a series of underground tunnels dug in the greensand under the middle of the town, supposedly once connected to the old abbey. There is a persistent story of buried treasure, hidden by the nuns to foil Thomas Cromwell and the commissioners; and to complete the picture, a ghostly monk is reputed to guard the treasure.

Further south, many places have tunnels connected to former smuggling activity. In Purbeck it is often hard to decide where stone quarrying tunnels end and smuggling hideaways begin; and the answer is that in many cases the holes had a dual purpose.

Many of the earthworks, barrows and historical sites that dot the Dorset landscape have been explored in the hope of finding buried treasure, often at the same time destroying valuable archaeological evidence; but some of the most surprising finds have come in very unlikely locations. In 1936 a Mr McIntyre was working on the building site of what is now Marks & Spencer in South Street, Dorchester. He discovered a bronze bowl and jar containing 22,000 Roman coins, dating back to the third century AD. This treasure can be seen in the Dorset County Museum in High West Street.

23

THE LANDLADY OF THE PILOT BOAT

Sit down, make yourselves at home – we pride ourselves on the welcome here. Nice dog, ma'am, if you don't mind me saying so; I had one just like her once. Cross-bred collie, if I'm not mistaken? Aye, she was a gem. Lassie – that was her name. That's her picture, up there on the wall.

The Pilot Boat? Oh, yes, 'tis an unusual name. Course, there's a lot of history in pub names, especially here in Dorset. Some of 'em go back hundreds of years, part of our island heritage, and for them that's interested, there's a great deal to be discovered from them. Take the Green Man – dozens of them, all over the country. Sometimes he's a woodsman; sometimes he's the outlaw Robin Hood himself; sometimes he's King Charles hiding in the oak tree, fleeing from the battle of Worcester; but more often than not, he's a real green man. The spirit of the trees – leaves coming out of his mouth, just like the foliate heads you find if you look carefully at the tops of pillars and around the roves of the older churches – a memory of the times when the old Gods were still remembered and revered.

Anyway, as I was saying: the Pilot Boat. Pilots used to go out to sea to help the bigger vessels into the harbour. Down near the seafront at Lyme, on stormy nights, the wind off the bay rattles the windows, and it's a daily job to clean the salt off the windows, we're that close to the sea. Busy in the summer of course, what with the tourists and the day trippers coming down on the train, not to mention all the geologists and fossil hunters down on the beach, chipping away at the cliffs, hoping to discover the next ancient monster, like Miss Anning did. Some of my regulars can't see much point in it – there's enough living fossils round here without digging up more dead ones they say – but give her her due, Miss Anning put the place on the map, and half the people here this time of year have come because of what she found. There's a pretty trade in old stone sea creatures, even if times are hard for them as catch the living fish.

Anyway, winter time is different. That's when the storms roll round and the big seas come, and then it's not such a picture postcard on Lyme seafront. But one particular night I shan't ever forget was the last day of December 1914. We still had the holly and ivy up round the windows, and we'd been busy all day – plenty of folk up on the cliffs with telescopes and binoculars, watching the navy. Proud sight it was, seven battleships in line ahead, steaming across the bay, HMS *Lord Nelson* in front and the good old *Formidable* bringing up the rear. Then there were the New Year's Eve revellers; despite the war, there was that feeling of warmth and optimism that always comes up as the New Year chimes in. It was a cold night; earlier in the evening it had been moonlit and clear, but towards midnight great storm clouds piled up on the horizon and we all knew we were in for a blow.

What we didn't know then, but soon found out, was that pretty much as the company in the Pilot Boat were singing 'Auld Lang Syne', a German torpedo struck the *Formidable* out in Lyme Bay, and she sank in the storm. She slid under so fast that her bow touched the bottom and she stood on

her head for a moment before she went under. Captain Loxley went down with his ship. He had an Airedale dog called Bruce, which was drowned alongside his master on the bridge. Well, the rescue boats from the cruisers around her did what they could, but the storm drove them back, and out of 780 men aboard, only 233 survived.

One boat ended up here in Lyme late the following night. By then we'd heard the news, so there was plenty down on the beach to throw a line and help the survivors ashore. Fifty were landed, but nine were dead or dying, and they were brought in here – laid out in the bar they was, just about where you're sitting. Aye, I shan't mind if I never see another drowned sailor, I can tell you …

Now to my mind, there are different sorts of stories – some true, just like what I've told you tonight; some completely made up from some chap's fertile imagination; and some that maybe start with truth and get shall we say wilder, or are complete fiction, but still have truth in them. So you can believe what I'm about to tell you or not, that's up to you.

Anyway, that was a bitter and sombre sight – nine sailors laid out in here, stiff and white, some was on the tables, and some was on coats on the floor. And then I noticed that Lassie was paying particular attention to one of the corpses, licking his hand; she wouldn't go away from him. When we looked closer, blessed if we didn't see signs of life, and the doctor who'd come down to pronounce 'em all dead set to it, and with brandy and the rubbing of his limbs he brought the dead to life. Well, wasn't that the best New Year gift that anyone could have wished for, there in the middle of such a disaster, one little spark of life and hope!

Able Seaman John Cowan was the sailor's name – a Scotsman – saved by my dog Lassie here, in the Pilot Boat; and that's as true as I'm sat here talking to you. It was in all the papers, even the London ones – not bad for business, I don't mind saying – and when he was fully recovered, John asked me for the dog, and of course I gave it to him. Inseparable, they were, and they do say that the dog's tale, if you'll pardon the pun, went all round the Empire. Some film makers in Hollywood got to hear of it, and dreamt up a whole series of yarns about a dog called Lassie – whether that's true or not, I can't rightly say. They never paid me a penny for the rights, that I do know. But that's why they say a dog is man's best friend, and there's no denying that fact. So that was the one bright thing in the whole sad business. Some of those poor sailors' bodies took a long time to come ashore, you know; almost the last was Bruce – Captain Loxley's dog. He was washed up at Abbotsbury some days later, and he's buried in the Gardens there. And if you don't believe me, go and see for yourself!

24

THE WONDERFUL CROCODILE

Come list ye landsmen all to me, to tell you the truth I'm bound,
What happened to me in going to sea and the wonders that
I found;
Shipwrecked I was one stormy night and cast upon the shore,
So I resolved to take a trip the country to explore

To my ri too ral oo ral ay, to my ri too ral ay
To my ri too ral liddle lol de fol
To my ri too ral ay

I walked along a month or so beside the mighty ocean,
And then I saw a something move, like all the world in
motion;
And coming near the monster's head, I saw 'twas a crocodile,
From the end of his nose to the tip of his tail he measured
twenty miles

This crocodile I could plainly see was none of the common
race
For he had to climb a very tall tree before I could see his face
There were horns upon his head my boys, they reached up to
the moon

A lad went up in January, and never got back 'til June

At length the wind began to blow a hurricane from the south
It swept me out of the coconut tree and into the croco-
dile's mouth
He quickly closed his jaws on me; he thought to gain a victim
But I ran down his throat you see, and that's the way I
tricked him ...

Down his gullet, mates, and do you know it was the size of
St Paul's Cathedral. There were two hundred choirboys all
singing, 'Don't Go down the Mine, Daddy' and a hundred
sextons ringing on the bells 'Ding dong, ding dong ...'

I went on a bit further, I came to his heart, it was the size of
the Tower of London, and there were a hundred despairing
lovers all weeping and throwing down their roses, saying it's
bigger than mine, it's bigger than mine ...

I went on a bit further, and I came to his lungs, they were
the size of hot air balloons, and when one went in, the other
went out in a roar of hot air like a Bessemer blast furnace,
and blew me right down to his vitals ...

I travelled on a year or so 'til I came to his maw,
And there were bread and cheese and apple trees, and barrels
of beer in store;
Right then I banished all my cares, for food I was not stinted,
And in that croc' I lived ten years very well contented ...

This crocodile being very old, at last the monster died
He was six months in turning cold; he was so thick and wide.
His skin was two miles thick I think, or very near abouts,

For I was a good six months my boys in digging myself out

I got out yesterday, and here I am. Now you may not believe this tale, but it's as true as I'm sitting here …

Some people think that song about the Wonderful Crocodile proves that there used to be crocodiles here in Dorset. And before you say that's a load of rubbish, think about those fossils that Mary Anning found in the cliffs at Lyme Regis.

Those plesiosaurs were great long beasts, with long jaws full of teeth, flippers on their sides, and a great tail behind, for all the world like crocodiles – so it might just be that the song is a faint echo of our Jurassic pre-history here in Dorset. Mind you, it could also be that the tale was brought here by the Irish navvies when the railways were being built in the 1850s; and it has to be said that the chorus does have a distinctly Irish flavour to it.

Tales of wildlife and the natural world abound in Dorset. Some are true, and even those that are not often have a kernel of truth in them. The sika deer that have bred so prolifically in Purbeck in recent years are not native to Dorset; their ancestors came from Japan, just over 100 years ago. They were brought to this country by Kenneth Robert Balfour who owned Brownsea Castle, and for several years they lived alongside the red squirrels on the island in Poole Harbour. In 1896 the castle was destroyed in a fire, and the sika deer escaped from the flames by swimming across the harbour to the Purbeck shore, where they rapidly established themselves.

The story goes that once a year all the stags in Purbeck meet on the top of Creech Grange; whether this is to agree territorial or herd rights for the following year is not clear!

Shapwick, near Wimborne, was once the scene of a terrible scare, and serves to underline how little most people moved around in the pre-railway days. The tenant farmers on the Bankes estate were in the habit of bringing seaweed inland on carts to fertilise their fields. One day, from one of the heaps of rotting weed, a dreadful monster emerged and terrorised the locals, who had no idea what it was. It was only when an old retired sailor came up to look at the creature that he was able to identify it as nothing worse than a crab. 'Shapwick crabs' was subsequently used as a term of ridicule in the area, but later on the villagers became rather proud of the story, and a farm in the village is called Crab Farm to this day.

Another true story concerns Major Radclyffe, a retired military gentleman. He was fishing for salmon in the lower reaches of the river Frome one day when a man came running up to tell him that there was a giant salmon in the pool further down the river. When the major enquired how big, the man replied that it was the biggest he had ever seen. The major was a man of his time, and he had fished and hunted big game all over the world and handled far larger creatures than the Frome was capable of supporting, so he was sceptical of the man's claims at first.

However, on arriving at the pool and seeing a large dorsal fin cutting the surface, and a large grey scaly back occasionally breaking through the water, the major was astonished to realise that the fish in question was a sturgeon. He'd caught them in Russian rivers, and the shape was unmistakable. It was also undoubtedly a very big fish indeed. His first thought was to shoot the fish, and no sooner said than done, he gave it both barrels with the shotgun he habitually carried whenever he ventured out into the country. This, however, made no impression on the fish, other than causing it to charge across the pool a few times and thrash its tail. Realising that stiffer measures were required, the major sent home for his elephant gun; but by the time the weapon arrived, the fish had prudently decided to slip beneath the water and seek a more peaceful part of the river.

That appeared to be that, until some weeks later, when news reached the major that the fish had been sighted again, in a weir pool further down the Frome. There was no point using bait, since the sturgeon is a bottom-feeding fish and was clearly not hungry. The major decided to attempt to hook the fish by grappling it, and proceeded to cast his line, weighted with several large hooks, until, at last, he succeeded in hooking the fish in the lower jaw. A tremendous battle commenced, during which the major and a stout friend were obliged to take turns on the rod, the strength of the fish being far superior to either of them. For an hour and forty-five minutes the contest continued until, following the suggestion of his bailiff, a man was sent to obtain a seine net. The giant fish was entangled in the net and brought to the bank, where it still required the work of three men and two large gaff hooks to get the fish out of the water.

The sturgeon measured 9ft 3in – as the major proudly remarked, 'Verily the largest fish ever captured with a rod and line in an English river.' As the fish was being dispatched on the riverbank, a local man came across the fields with a towel over his arm and the intention of going for a swim in the river. He stared at the fish and remarked, 'Lor, zur, do 'ee think there be any more like that in there, 'cos if so I bain't going in!' Despite the major's opinion that it was extremely unlikely, and that in any case the sturgeon was not carnivorous, the man decided that discretion was the better part of valour, and went for a bicycle ride instead. The deceased sturgeon was photographed tied onto the roof of Major Radclyffe's motor car, with his four daughters sitting on the running boards. It can be inspected in the Dorset County Museum.

As with all fishermen's tales, however, there is an even bigger one. It comes from Dorset's other main river, the Stour. The fish in question was a pike, hooked by an angler in the mill pool at Sturminster Newton. The pike was so large that he had to play the fish all the way down the river to Wimborne before he could find a place wide enough and turn the fish around to bring it back to Sturminster. And that's a real fisherman's tale.

25

THERE'S ONLY THEE AND ME IN THE ROOM

Well, back that time o' day there were lots of old inns on lonely roads. I suppose they were roads that used to be busy at one time, but when the new turnpikes came in, they were not used so much as before; except on fairs and feast days, when all the old farmers and countrymen came out, and took the routes that they'd used all their lives. This particular hostelry was in the bleakest spot you could imagine, perched on the brow of a hill where the wind whistled constantly, and the whole place was often wreathed in cloud. One cold winter's day a traveller was hurrying along the road. It started to snow, and before long the snow started to pitch and slowed him right down, and he realised he would never make his destination before night. Just when he was beginning to think he might have to find a barn to bed down in for the night, he saw a light ahead, and when he got closer he was relieved to see it was this old inn. There were lights in the windows, and all kinds of carts and wagons in the yard, and it looked busy and cheerful.

He went into the bar, shaking the snow off his coat, ordered a drink and asked the barmaid if he could book a room for the night. 'I'm sure you can, dearie,' she replied cheerfully, 'I'll go and ask.' She disappeared into the room behind the bar, where the landlord was sitting at the table writing in a great ledger. The weary traveller was disappointed to see the landlord look up at the girl's question and shake his head, pointing at the page. She came back out, full of apologies. 'I'm really sorry,' she said, 'landlord says we're full up. Market day in Bridport tomorrow, see.'

The traveller was desperate. 'Could I have a word with the landlord please?' he asked.

The landlord came out, bringing the book. 'Very sorry sir,' he said. 'No room at all tonight.'

'What about that little room at the back, Mr Brown?' said the barmaid.

'Oh no, not at all suitable, not for a gentleman such as this,' the landlord replied. The traveller looked out of the window; the snow was falling thicker than ever. He begged the landlord to let him use the room.

The landlord leaned over the bar and beckoned to the traveller. In a whisper, he said, 'I don't want it known, because it might hurt trade, and God knows it's hard enough to keep this place running. That room's haunted, that's why we don't let it out; no one can sleep in it because of the ghost.'

The traveller scoffed, and said brightly, 'Well you can hire it to me for this evening Landlord. I don't believe in ghosts. I never saw anything at night much worse than myself, so I'll be pleased to spend the night in that room, and then you'll be able to let the room just like all the rest, because I will have proved it's not haunted.'

'Very well sir, if you say so,' said the landlord, but he didn't look convinced. 'Just don't blame me or my inn if you can't sleep a wink.'

The traveller had a hearty meal in front of the fire, and went to bed in the best of spirits. The sheets were clean, and it was only a matter of minutes before he was fast asleep.

In the middle of the night, however, he woke up. The room felt cold and he had the strangest feeling that someone else was in the bed with him. He felt himself begin to sweat, and then he heard a small voice whispering, 'There's only thee and me in the room!'

He pulled the covers over his head and tried to ignore what he'd heard.

Again the voice said, 'There's only thee and me in the room!'

By now the traveller was fully awake, and trembling under the bedclothes.

The voice spoke again, louder this time, 'There's only thee and me in the room!'

The traveller leapt out of bed, saying, 'Thee wait 'til I've got me boots on, then there'll only be thee!' and he was off down those stairs and out of that inn like lightning.

Oh yes, there's plenty of people round here will tell you tales of things that go bump in the night, like the black dog in Dark Lane out near Ibberton, and another one round Hod Hill, and Roman soldiers marching up on top of the old fort. I've even heard people say that Sheep Hill in Blandford is haunted by a ghostly ram – a white one I dare say, most of them are round here. Old Fred Blandford used to say that at midnight on New Year's Eve, the greyhound dogs that sit atop Lord Portman's gateposts come down and go for a drink in the Stour.

Out at Tarrant Gunville they have two stories. One is about Albert Philips, who milked a dairy there. One night he was driving the cows home from Bloody Shard Gate when he felt something tapping him on the shoulder; when he looked 'twas a hand all dripping with blood, pointing down the road towards Pimperne. Proper shook him up it did, and when he told the vicar he said that in the Civil War between King and Parliament, a King's man got his hand cut off at that very place, and 'twas buried in a little casket in Pimperne Churchyard.

The other tale from Tarrant is that a ghostly carriage pulled by headless horses is meant to tear along the road from Langton Long to Gunville, where at one time there was a great house. Eastbury House it was called, biggest house in the whole of Dorset – this is going back 150 years, mind. It's nearly all gone now; there is only the stable block left, and that's a lot bigger than your average mansion. Anyway, this carriage is supposed to be driven by the ghost of the steward, who was cheating his master out of all his money; and when his treachery was about to be revealed, he raced back to try to destroy the evidence. When he couldn't, he hanged himself, and that's why, they say, his ghost keeps walking – or riding, rather! Myself, I reckon most of these so-called ghost stories are nothing more than yarns put about by the smugglers to keep people off the roads at night, so as they could run their contraband unnoticed. There was plenty of that went on round here, and that is the truth!

Mind you, there was one thing happened here a few years ago that no one has ever managed to explain. No, not even Revd Anderson, the schoolmaster and Lord Portman, and I reckon between the three of 'em, they got the most brains in this neighbourhood. What I'm going to tell 'ee, I know is the truth, because I knew the house myself, and my sister lived in the village where the tale ended. This is what happened.

I worked at the time as gardener for a lady called Mrs Best up at Norden, on the edge of Durweston. Kindly soul she was, and often took in lodgers. Well, one autumn the Misses Pitt over at Steepleton House, who were always doing good works as you might say, got Mrs Best to take in

two workhouse girls; one of 'em was thirteen and the other
was four. These girls had only been in the cottage a few
days when strange things began to happen: at first it was
only little knocks and scratching sounds, not much more
than mice really. But soon the noises got worse until it was
like someone was hitting the walls with a sledgehammer.
Stones were thrown through the windows, and then flew
back out again; and all the cups and plates would fly off
the shelves of their own accord. Why, I was up there one
Tuesday planting some onion sets in the back garden, and
Mrs Best came out in tears saying, 'Oh dear dear, John,
I really don't know what to do; I'm not safe in my own
house.' And then there was a crash, and that was a basin
broken on the floor. The strange thing was, whenever those
girls were out at school, or gone visiting, or playing up in

the woods or down by the Stour, it didn't happen – it was only when they were under that roof.

In the end Mrs Best sent for the rector, and he came on up, but he was as flummoxed as the rest of us. The day he came in, he was sitting in the parlour taking a cup of tea, talking to the two girls as polite as you like, when there was a crash out the back, and that was another window broke. Instinctively he looked up, and there, above his head, was a great brown stain spreading all over the ceiling, like as if someone had dropped an oil lamp upstairs and the oil had seeped through the floorboard and the plaster. Well, then the rector went up to see Lord Portman, and they went to see the schoolmaster, and all three of them came up to Mrs Best's, but they were all at a loss to explain what might be the cause of it.

Lord Portman was anxious to keep it out of the newspapers, and in favour of quietly getting one of his London friends down to investigate it. Well, back then his word was law, so that was what was done; none less than the Duke of Argyll and his friends from the Psychical Research Society arrived down. They brought this medium fella with them to get in touch with the troubled spirits, whoever or whatever they might be, and one of these so-called spirits told 'em that there was treasure buried in the garden. Well, that done it, of course. Word got round quicker than measles, and there was all sorts turned up here wanting to dig for it in my garden; couple of fellows from Stourpaine got in one night and ruined a good crop of runners and half my cabbages too, and of course, found nothing at all. But it was curious, there's no denying that. Mrs Best was at her wits' end, and the only thing to do was to see if it would make any difference by moving the girls out of the cottage. So in the end they went down to live with Mr Cross in Durweston, and blowed if the same sort of malarkey didn't start happening there too.

Well, after that the Misses Pitt had them sent up to stay in another place in Iwerne Minster – my sister Annie was in service with Mr Ismay at Clayesmore House at the time, that's how I know. And 'twas the same thing up there, bangings and bumpings, and plaster coming off the walls. In the end there was nothing for it but to send the girls back to London. I was sorry for them; they were polite little creatures, sickly both of 'em, but you'd never have thought they could raise such a stir, and they seemed as bewildered as everyone else by the business.

So that's it – explain it if you can. I don't believe in ghosts, but neither can I tell you the cause of what happened to Mrs Best; and nor could the rector, or the schoolmaster, or Lord Portman.

The events at Durweston took place in the winter of 1894. I have two personal connections with the tale. My late father-in-law Geoffrey Spencer, who spent most of his adult life in Iwerne Minster, knew of the story and believed it to be true, as did a family friend, Mrs Cake. In their time, the house in Iwerne where the poltergeist activity had taken place was owned by a Mrs Forde, and the story was still remembered in the 1970s. In around 2000, I was working on a music project in the Day Centre at Castleman House in Blandford Forum, where I met two ladies from Durweston who knew the story well. One of the ladies was the daughter of Mrs Best's gardener. Fred Blandford, melodeon player and storyteller, was a resident at that time. I lent him a melodeon to play, as his had been washed away down the Stour after he left it one night in a riverside pub, and the river rose and flooded all the houses in East Street.

THE MUMMERS

Christmas Eve 1827 was a night to remember in Fordington. The regulars at the Union Arms reckoned they'd never known a Christmas like it. It all began earlier that day in James Burt's woodshed. The old Waterloo soldier had been laid off from the

brickyard where he worked down by the Frome earlier that week due to the frost, and the cold had sharpened since then. He'd set to and found his old sabre, and pinned some rags on his hat brim and jacket, and put a can of cider on the fire to warm up. One by one the rest of the mummers had arrived. Joseph Lock, who was to play the Turkish Knight, came coughing through the door, sat by the fire, took a pull from the cider, and began to rub his face with a burnt cork to blacken it; next was Joe Lucas, with his tool bag emptied of all but a ferocious-looking saw and a claw hammer, and a small bottle of rum for the hokum-pokum elecampane.

'Hereheis, JamesBurt, anddon'tyoubelettinghimgetdrunk or disgracing himself like he did last year.' They all cringed. It was Mary Hammet and her poor husband William, who played Little Jolly Jack, though a less jolly Jack could scarcely be found anywhere in Fordington. The man was hardly able to breathe without permission from his wife, but they kept him on in the mummers out of sympathy for his predica-ment, and a feeling that, at least once a year, it was good for a man to have a little freedom. Mary strode over to the cider can, and took a big pull.

'Too strong,' she announced, 'make sure he don't have too much of that.' And with that she was off into the dark towards the Union Arms.

'And a merry Christmas to you too, ma'am,' said the old soldier reflectively. Brother George was the last to arrive, and it was clear that he hadn't come straight from home, but had felt the need to fortify himself on the way. James was vexed; he liked to run a tight ship with the mummers (it was his mili-tary training showing through), and such a carefree attitude towards the night's proceedings didn't go down well with him.

'We're all hard up,' he said grimly, 'and if we don't match what we took last year, it'll be short rations for us all – and that'll be your fault, George.' George looked suitably abashed, stuck a sprig of holly in his hat, and picked up the bell.

'In comes I, Wold Father Christmas …' he began, and the rehearsal was underway, an hour late maybe, but very much the same as it had been for as long as any of them could remember, right back to the year 1816, when Corporal Burt came back in triumph to Dorchester from Waterloo, and took over the mummers from his father. For as long as anyone could remember, the Burts and their friends had done the mummers in Fordington at Christmas; they were known for it, and regarded it as their right.

When the words were said over, and all the Doctor's crazy business was seen to, they turned to the sword fight. This was the corporal's speciality: he still cut a fine figure in his role as St George, and he prided himself on the fact that they used real swords, one of which had drawn French blood on many occasions – although perhaps not quite so many as he now remembered. The ring of the cold steel in the frosty air sobered them all, and they gathered up their bags, swords and bell, and set off for the town.

'First off we'll go to the doctor's; he's got guests in tonight and we're sure of a welcome there; then the pub, then the green, after that Farmer Swingler, and then the new vicar's to finish off. Look lively, but go quiet, so as not to give the game away!'

They took one final swig, and the cider can was replenished and set at the back of the fire to warm them on their return.

When they arrived at the doctor's, the corporal strode boldly up to the door and knocked. The mummers formed up ready to begin as the door opened. They waited, and waited, but no one came. The corporal frowned, 'Can't understand it,' he muttered, 'I saw the doctor only this morning; I know we're a bit late, thanks to George – but not that late …'

He knocked on the door with his sabre. At last the doctor's manservant came to the door. 'Fordington mummers sir, as usual,' said the corporal.

'What d'you mean, as usual?' said the man, surveying the band with distaste. 'D'you think you can come round here imposing yourselves on the doctor's hospitality twice in an evening, and on Christmas Eve? Clear off before I call the constable.'

'But we're expected,' said the corporal.

'Expected be damned; you're all so drunk you can't remember where you've been; be off with you.' And with that, the door was unceremoniously slammed in their faces.

The dismayed mummers looked at each other blankly; this was not the start they'd hoped for. 'Never mind,' said the corporal. 'Chin up mates; never say die. Let's try the Union.'

That cheered them all up, because if there was one place in Fordington they were assured of a warm welcome and plenty of ale, even if the financial benefits were not usually great, it was the tavern. Off they went through the streets, and as they approached the Union Arms, George began to ring his bell furiously. They burst in through the door, and Father Christmas launched into his time-honoured opening speech. 'In comes I, Wold Father Christmas, welcome or welcome not.'

'Welcome not,' said a voice, and there was a gale of laughter, and catcalls, and other exclamations that were not at all of a seasonal nature; and above the hubbub Mary Hammet's shrill voice crowing, 'Oh my dear Lor', they're so drunk, they don't know where they've been, and it's only nine o'clock!'

The corporal rose to the occasion, pulled himself up to his full height and brandished his sword. 'Now look here,' he said, 'we're come here to do the mummers, and by God we'll carry it through!'

The landlord pushed his way to the front and squared up to St George. 'Come off it, James,' he said, 'a joke's a joke, but you can't do the play twice in the same place on the same night; 'tidden right, you know that. Now off you go, the lot of you, and don't impose on my customers, for I won't have it!' This was greeted by ringing cheers from the delighted topers, and the mummers were forced into an ignominious retreat. They made their way round the corner and stopped to lick their wounds.

'Twice in one night – I don't like it; 'tis an omen,' said Little Jolly Jack lugubriously.

'Omen be damned,' said the corporal angrily, 'someone else is taking our place, and mumming where we should be mumming, damned if they bain't!'

On they went down the road towards Farmer Swingler. On the way, the corporal noticed something lying in the road. He stooped down to examine the object, and picked up a string or rag tatters on the end of his sabre. He looked behind at his fellow mummers. None of them had rags of the same colour or material pinned on their coats; a horrible suspicion was beginning to form in his mind.

'Aha,' he said again. 'Someone else is taking our place, and mumming where we should be mumming, damned if they bain't!'

Just at that moment they heard the unmistakable sound of a bass drum in the distance, echoing round the narrow streets and getting louder as it approached. 'Quick,' said the corporal, 'hide in Jenner's yard!'

All the mummers disappeared behind the tall wooden gates of the builders' merchants' premises, and peeped through the cracks and knotholes in the old timbers. They were just in time to see a party of five mummers, clad almost identically to themselves, swaggering up the street. One of them was beating frantically on a great drum.

'Well, I'll be …' said George, rubbing his eyes, 'there I be in front, Father Christmas, and all the rest of you behind me, and yet here I be too – I should never have had so much to drink, and I heartily repent of it. Never again will I allow a drop of the demon liquor to …'

'Oh, for goodness' sake, shut your row,' said his brother hoarsely. 'Can't you see what 'tis? 'Tis others taking our place and stealing our rightful work.'

'Aye, that's right James,' said the Turkish Knight, 'and I know who it is.'

They all looked at him in amazement. How could he have possibly identified them, disguised as they were in hats and tatter coats?

''Tis they Keates from up Bockhampton, and John Hardy, I'll swear to it.'

'That's as maybe, but how can you tell?' said the corporal, somewhat put out at not being the one to offer this revela-tory news himself.

'I overheard John Hardy ask Benjamin Barratt for the loan of the Scorpion Band drum for a bit of Christmas musicking he was planning with his neighbours; and that's the drum – we all know it.'

They did. Of course they knew it; it was a famous drum. It was the biggest and loudest in south Dorset, and was reputed to have single-handedly repelled a whole brigade of Frenchmen on the road to Valenciennes.

Once again the corporal rose to the occasion. 'Come on,' he said fiercely, 'we'll not be beaten by the likes of them. They won't know where to go next. Off to the vicar's.'

So they made their way towards the new vicarage, to enter-tain the reverend gentleman. He had expressed an interest in seeing the custom, purely from an antiquarian point of view, and had invited several like-minded clerics and their wives around for a small glass of seasonal cheer and a short diversion before the serious business of their midnight services began.

As they walked up the gravel of the carriage drive, the corporal felt his nerve begin to fail him; but Father Christmas, now sobered by the evening's events, strode boldly up to the door, which was decorated with a great wreath of holly and ivy, and rang the bell. At length the vicar appeared, looking annoyed.

'Really, Mr Burt, that is outrageous,' he said severely. 'Not only do you perform a play for my guests that contained many scurrilous and blasphemous words, so that I was obliged to send the ladies indoors and hope that the worst of the offence was masked by the coarseness of your dialect, but you have the nerve to come back again, despite my express instructions not to do so.'

The corporal protested. 'It wasn't we, yer worship,' he said piteously. 'It was others, taking our place unlawfully.'

'Come, come Mr Burt, you can't expect me to believe that. Now away with you all, and do not tempt my patience further. I expect to see you all in church later on this evening.' And with that, he went back into the vicarage, and another door was shut in their faces.

The corporal's blood was now up. He turned to his men. 'Come on,' he said, 'we'll find those varmints and put a stop to their thieving activities. Follow me.'

'Maybe we should just go back home and forget about it for this year,' said the Turkish Knight.

'What, and lose our rights to those scoundrels? They've got to be taught a lesson; otherwise we'll be the laughing stock of the place, and never able to show our faces inside the Union Arms again.'

This was a prospect too awful to countenance, so off they went. They came to the green and heard the drum thumping away in the distance.

'Hello St George, fancy seeing you again; coming in?' cooed a voice from a doorway. They all stopped and stared. It was Nance Mogridge, a lady well known to all of them.

'Oh, er, good evening Nancy, and, er merry Christmas,' said the corporal awkwardly.

'Oh yes, merry Christmas,' said Nance, 'and as it is Christmas, why not come in again?'

'Again?' said the corporal. 'What d'you mean?'

'James Burt, shame on you. Have you had that much to drink that you can't remember, you naughty boy? You was here less than an hour ago.'

And then the penny dropped. 'St George was it?' enquired the corporal gruffly.

'Oh yes,' said Nance merrily. 'What a big sword you've got.'

'Wooden or metal?' inquired the old soldier.

'Wooden,' said the lady, 'but painted up silver very nicely.'

'Ha,' said the corporal, producing his sabre with a flourish, 'then it weren't me. We've been impersonated Nancy, and them that's done it have got to pay.'

'Hooray!' said the lady, scenting a showdown. 'Shall I tell the rest of 'em at the Union?'

'Yes,' said the corporal decisively, 'Gray's Bridge in ten minutes. Follow me!'

Meanwhile their rivals, who were more than a little merry, and whose pockets were full with coins, cheese and cake, were making their way unsteadily towards the river. They were congratulating themselves on the complete success of their evening. The songs and carols had been well received, the Scorpion's drum had played its part in attracting good crowds wherever they'd been, and in addition they had sampled all the delights of Fordington until they could hardly stand. It wasn't until the corporal, the Fordington mummers and the denizens of the Union Arms were almost upon them – when it was far too late to run for it – that they realised that their incursion into enemy territory had been rumbled.

The corporal was in his element. 'Charge!' he shouted. 'Remember the Duke! Never say die!' And with that, battle was closed, and the greatest fight seen in the town since the last parliamentary elections took place, on Gray's Bridge, as Christmas Day approached.

The two Doctors ended up in the Frome, the two Jolly Jacks took to their heels across the water meadows, and John Hardy sloped off back to Bockhampton, almost hidden by the Scorpion's drum. Back on the bridge the St Georges and the Turkish Knights battled it out royally, cheered on by the drunken mob. At last, however, the corporal's cavalry sabre won the day; his rival's sword splintered, and Joseph Keates' head was dealt a glancing blow, and he fell bleeding to the ground. Suddenly the mood of the crowd changed. 'He shouldn't have done that, oh dear, no, weren't fair; Joseph only had a wooden sword.'

The corporal looked down at his rival, and knew that, although he had won the battle, he had lost the war. He walked to the edge of the bridge, flung his sword into the river, squared his shoulders and walked calmly through the silent throng, up through the town to the gaol and knocked at the door. And that was the last time the Fordington mummers ever appeared in Fordington at Christmastide.

The *Dorset County Chronicle* of 24 January 1828 reported that John Locke, Joseph Lucas, and James and George Burt were all indicted for causing a riot on 24 December, and that James Burt maliciously wounded James Keates. They were found guilty. James Burt was sentenced to six months with hard labour, while the other three got three months with hard labour.

It must be remembered that although the story seems comic now, at the time wages for agricultural labourers were very bad, and most of the inhabitants of Fordington lived in appalling conditions. Outbreaks of machine-breaking and incendiarism were not uncommon, and conditions were in place locally that would lead to the tragic events at Tolpuddle six years later. Mumming and carolling at Christmas time was a serious business, and the small amount of money realised would have made a big difference to the families involved. The severity of the sentences handed down reflects the harshness of the criminal code at the time, and the nervousness of the ruling classes at any semblance of unrest.

Christmas mumming was a significant part of Yuletide celebration in Dorset all through the nineteenth century, right up to the present time. Plays are mentioned in Wool, Corfe, Evershot and West Lulworth. Thomas Hardy memorably incorporated one into Mrs Wildeve's Christmas party in *The Return of the Native*. William Barnes' poem 'The Humstrum' records the sound of a primitive home-made rebec-like instrument used by mummers in the Blackmore Vale. The BBC recorded a Dorchester play in the 1950s, and then filmed the celebrated Symondsbury Mummer's Play, which is alive and well and can still be seen in the Bridport area in and around Christmas time.

WILLIAM AND THE BULL

William was the best fiddler in the area, known all around as the man for the job when it came to dances and celebrations where music was required. So when Timothy Thomas got married to Sarah Rose, it was the most natural thing in the world to ask old William to play. Now this all happened one glorious summer's day at the end of June, just after midsummer. But to understand what happened after, I must just make sure that you know of the old West Country belief that at midnight on Christmas Eve, if you go into a stable or a barn, or anywhere where beasts are kept, you will see them on their knees, in honour of the birth of Jesus. Down in Somerset they also say that at that special time, midnight on Christmas Eve, beasts can talk; but that may be due to the scrumpy they drink in those parts …

Anyway, on the day of the wedding all the folks went to church, and there was old William sat in the gallery playing sacred music on the violin; and whenever the vicar called for a hymn or psalm, old William led them all in the singing most appropriately. The service being over and the couple wed, the bride and groom linked arms in the traditional way and led the congregation out of the church and down towards the tithe barn, with old William in front, playing the 'Caledonian March' or 'Bonaparte's Retreat'.

When they got to the barn, it looked beautiful. Walls freshly whitewashed, floor swept, greenery around the windows and doors, great long tables down the middle all groaning with eatables and drinkables. They all sat down and the feasting began – all except for old William, who was perched on a barrel over to one side, playing lively song tunes and ditties to keep 'em all humming while they ate. But they didn't forget him, oh no. Because in Dorset, folk are very hospitable towards musicians; you only have to hear the string of a fiddle or the toot of a flute, and you can't help yourself. You have to dip your hand in your pocket and give them a few pence, or something to eat, or maybe a drink; so as William played, someone gave him some beef, someone else gave him some cake; someone else gave him some beer and someone else gave him some cider – so he was fed and watered as he played.

After two or three hours the food was all gone, so they cleared away the tables, pushed the benches to the walls and began to dance. They did the longways dances and the circle dances, the right-hand stars and the do-si-dos, and there was old William sawing away on the fiddle, playing 'Up the Sides and Down the Middle', and all the jigs and reels and horn-pipes popular in that neighbourhood at the time. As he played someone gave him some gin, someone else gave him some whisky, someone else gave him some rum, and someone else (who should have known better) gave him a glass of brandy. So consequently, when the bride and groom had gone off on honeymoon, and all the guests had gone home, the only person left in the barn was old William, absolutely exhausted – well he'd been playing all day – and, to tell you the truth, not completely sober. So he made a mistake, which, had he been in his usual state of mind, he never would have made – he took a short cut across Long Meadow.

Now, anyone in the village would have told you that this was where the farmer kept his bull. But William had forgotten this; at least, he forgot it until he was as far as he could possibly be from any of the four hedges. And then, in the darkness, he heard a pounding of hooves and the sound of heavy snorting; and looking round, he saw Farmer Chick's prize bull Captain, charging towards him in the moonlight, horns a-glinting.

Well, William was far too tired to run for it, so in the circumstances he did the only sensible thing; he took up his fiddle and began to play. Well, it was very lucky for William that Captain was musical; as soon as he heard the music he stopped, listened, and a contented smile came over his face; and as long as William kept playing, all was well. As soon as he stopped to think of another tune, down went the bull's head, and his hooves began pawing the ground – so William had to keep playing.

He played all his jigs and reels and hornpipes; he played them all again; then he even played a waltz or two. The night wore on, until at last, William had one of those dreadful moments that all musicians experience, when you know that you know more tunes, but you can't remember what they are. And down went Captain's head, and his hooves were pawing on the ground … and then William had a flash of inspiration. Even though it was the middle of June, he very slowly and reverently began to play the old Nativity hymn, 'While Shepherds Watched Their Flocks by Night'.

Well, it was very lucky for William that not only was Captain musical, he was also religious. He thought it must be Christmas Eve, so down he went on his great knees, and down went his head until his horns were touching the ground. William took his chance, took to his heels and was over the hedge before the bull could get up again. And as he said afterwards, he'd often seen people look stupid, but he'd never seen a bull look stupid before; and that's the story of William and the Bull.

The violin or fiddle was the pre-eminent instrument for village music in Dorset until the arrival of melodeons and concertinas in the middle of the nineteenth century. Thomas Hardy

played the violin and loved country dancing; his father, uncle
and grandfather all played string instruments, and formed the
nucleus of the church band in Stinsford parish church just
outside Dorchester. Their collection of dance tunes, handwritten in the back of their carol books, has long formed the
basis of the repertoire of local céilí bands. Hardy was fasci-
nated with stories connected to fiddles and fiddle playing, and
included them in many of his poems and novels; a short version of William and the Bull is told by dairyman Crick in *Tess
of the d'Urbervilles*.

The dialect poems of William Barnes, based largely on
childhood memories of north Dorset and the Blackmore
Vale, contain many references to fiddle music at local celebrations. Recently, the music manuscript of Benjamin Rose,
a farmer, alehouse keeper and fiddle player from Belchalwell,
has emerged. It is dated 1820, and contains 133 country
dance tunes of the sort that old William would have played
to Captain. Here's one of them, 'Jack's Alive':

BIBLIOGRAPHY

Briggs, K.M., *A Dictionary of British Folk Tales in the English Language* (Routledge & Kegan Paul, 1970)

Dewar, H.L.S, *The Dorset Ooser, Dorset Monographs No.2* (Dorset Natural History and Archaeological Society, 1968)

Dorset Federation of Women's Institutes, *Dorset Within Living Memory* (Countryside Books, 1996)

Dorset Federation of Women's Institutes, *Hidden Dorset* (Countryside Books, 1990)

Dorset Federation of Women's Institutes, *Dorset Up Along and Down Along* (1948)

English Nature, *Hartland Moor* (English Nature, 2004)

Hyland, P., *Purbeck: The Ingrained Island* (The Dovecot Press, 1978)

Innes, B., *Shaftesbury: An Illustrated History* (The Dovecot Press, 1992)

Jackson, M.A., *The History of the Dorset Button* (Borcombe Printers, 1970)

Knot, O., *Witches of Wessex* (Self-published)

Legg, R., *Bridport and Lyme Regis* (Dorset Publishing Co., 1999)

Oliver, C., *Myths and Legends of the Saxon Saints of Wimborne* (Unknown)

Palmer, K., *Oral Folk Tales of Wessex* (David & Charles, 1973)

Udal, J.S., *Dorsetshire Folk-Lore* (Dorset Books, 1989)